Alma Holman Burton

Four American Patriots

Patrick Henry. Alexander Hamilton, Andrew Jackson, Ulysses S. Grant

Alma Holman Burton

Four American Patriots
Patrick Henry. Alexander Hamilton, Andrew Jackson, Ulysses S. Grant

ISBN/EAN: 9783337308117

Printed in Europe, USA, Canada, Australia, Japan

Cover: Foto ©ninafisch / pixelio.de

More available books at **www.hansebooks.com**

FOUR AMERICAN PATRIOTS

PATRICK HENRY   ALEXANDER HAMILTON

ANDREW JACKSON   ULYSSES S. GRANT

A BOOK FOR YOUNG AMERICANS

BY ALMA HOLMAN BURTON

WERNER SCHOOL BOOK COMPANY

NEW YORK   **CHICAGO**   BOSTON

CONTENTS

THE STORY OF PATRICK HENRY

THE STORY OF ALEXANDER HAMILTON

THE STORY OF ANDREW JACKSON

THE STORY OF ULYSSES S. GRANT.

THE STORY OF

PATRICK HENRY

PATRICK HENRY.

THE STORY OF PATRICK HENRY.

I.—CHILDHOOD.

Patrick Henry was born on the 29th of May, 1736, in Hanover County, Virginia. George Washington was born on the 22d of February, 1732, in Westmoreland County.

While one was a baby rocking in his cradle, the other was still so small that he played about in dresses like a girl.

Many years later these Virginia boys were great friends, and, as we shall see, they became two of the most famous men in the history of our country.

The blue-eyed Patrick grew very fast. When he was old enough to go about alone, he found playmates in the woods.

The birds sang to him, the fishes dared him to dive into the clear water after them, and the bees often droned about him until he fell asleep on the grass.

Patrick's father was a Scotchman from Aberdeen, and some of his father's people were scholars of such renown that they were known throughout Europe.

He told the boy all about these noted ancestors, and started a private school to encourage him to study to make a great man of himself.

But Patrick did not care very much for books. He liked to guide a canoe down the South Anna River, which ran past the little farm where he lived. He spent many hours on the green bank watching the cork of his fishing rod. He often wandered far into the forest to set traps for the game. And you can easily guess that his lessons were never very well prepared.

His mother always took him to the Presbyterian church to hear Mr. Davies preach.

Mr. Davies was a wonderful man. He was tall and erect. His face was beautiful, and his manners were so polished that some one said he seemed like the embassador of a great king.

At church Patrick kept his eyes wide open and listened to every word the preacher said. When he returned home, his mother would ask him to give the text and repeat all of the sermon he could.

Patrick loved to imitate the clear, sweet voice and graceful gestures of Mr. Davies. His mother said she hoped he would make a preacher.

But his father said he did not like books well enough for that. At last he said he believed the boy would never be a scholar, and that he was only fit for some kind of trade. So he sent him to live with a merchant, that he might learn how to buy and sell goods.

II.—The Young Merchant.

After Patrick had clerked for a year, his father bought some tea and coffee and spices, some woolen and cotton cloths, and some tin and iron ware from a British trader. Then he gave all that he had bought to Patrick and his elder brother, William, to set up business for themselves.

The boys were very proud of their new shop. They swept it out and dusted it every morning, and put samples of their goods in the window where the light streamed through many small panes of glass.

Now, the shop was not in a city nor even in a village. It was on the edge of their father's small farm.

For miles around there were large farms or plantations, each with a fine house where a planter lived. About the houses clustered the log cabins of the negro slaves. Farther off in the skirts of the forest stood the huts of the poor whites.

The place was rather lonesome for business. Sometimes a fine coach stopped at the little shop and a pompous planter made a purchase. But the rich did not buy much there. They traded at their own wharves with the British merchants who came in shallops up the river.

They exchanged bales of tobacco for boxes and barrels of goods which they kept in the store-rooms of their houses. The slaves did not buy anything, for their masters clothed and fed them. It was only the small farmers and the poor whites who lived from hand to mouth that traded with the Henry boys.

This class of people did not have much money. They often paid their bills by making friendly visits. They lounged about the shop telling stories, cracking jokes, and quarreling with one another.

Patrick lay on the counter watching them. He did not talk much himself, but when he returned home he amused the rest of the family by screwing his face around and changing his voice until he looked and spoke like each one of his customers.

As the days went by, the boys found it very tiresome waiting for trade. William went sometimes behind the shelves to drink from a bottle of rum. Patrick never drank rum. When he heard the birds calling, he skipped away for a tramp through the woods.

If he chanced to see the tracks of deer, he followed them far into the underbrush. Perhaps he returned after several hours to find his brother asleep and somebody waiting to buy a penny's worth of something.

Of course, business could not be a success when carried on in that way. Before the year was out the brothers found their goods all gone and their shop closed up.

William went more and more to a grog shop,

and became a very worthless fellow indeed. But Patrick was kind and gentle in his manners ; he played well on the violin and was a great favorite with the young people in the neighborhood.

And so the years passed by, and he grew up to be a tall young man, without having learned any useful business whereby he might earn a living through honest labor.

III.—The Farm and the Shop.

Patrick won the love of a bright-eyed little lass who had bought many a ha'penny worth of his peppermints. He was poor, and so was she; but he said by putting their shoulders together they might be better able to bear their poverty.

He was only eighteen, and she was younger still; but he said that their ages together made over thirty years. That sounded very old indeed! And so without a dollar in his pocket Patrick Henry married little Sarah Shelton.

Patrick's father gave him a small patch of land, and Sarah's father gave her two or three slaves to set up house keeping with.

The tall Virginia boy went into the tobacco field with his negroes. He dressed in homespun and looked like a farmer; and when the neighbors rode past, they smilingly said, "That boy of John Henry's is finding out how to work."

Patrick worked hard on week days. When Sunday came, he always went to church.

Like his father, he was an Episcopalian, but he loved so well to hear Mr. Davies preach that he attended the Presbyterian church.

One Sunday in May, 1755, Mr. Davies talked about war.

The country north of the Ohio River belonged to the English colonies, yet the French from Canada were building forts there to keep the English away.

King George had sent General Braddock to America with an army of grenadiers, and a Virginia regiment was marching to join him.

They would go to the Ohio country and drive out the French.

Patrick wished very much that he might be a soldier and help fight for the king. But the wife and babies must be fed, and so he toiled on in the field with the negroes.

One Sunday in August Mr. Davies looked very sad when he rose to preach.

He said that news had just come from the Ohio country. General Braddock had been killed and his army defeated. Many brave Virginia boys lay dead on the field of battle.

Yet, he said, a Virginia officer named George Washington, had saved a part of the army.

"Colonel Washington," said Mr. Davies, "is only twenty-three years old. I cannot but hope that Providence has preserved the youth in so signal a manner for some important service to his country."

"Ah," thought Patrick, "George Washington has done so much for his country, and he is only twenty-three!"

He looked down at his hands. They were brown and rough with toil.

"Alas!" he said, "I do my best, and yet I cannot even make a living on my little farm!"

This was quite true.

Patrick could not make his crops grow. Then his house caught fire and burned to the ground. It was all very discouraging!

He thought, if he tried once more, he might succeed as a merchant. So he sold his slaves, and with the money which they brought he built a house and purchased a small stock of goods.

That very year the tobacco crop failed. People were not able to pay for what they bought. There was nothing to do but wait for the next crop.

Meantime Patrick's shop became the lounging place for the whole neighborhood.

The small planters and overseers dropped in to talk about crops. The trappers from beyond the Blue Ridge Mountains stopped with their packs of furs to tell of the Indians on the frontiers.

The ferrymen who paddled the boats across the river repeated the latest gossip of the Yankee peddlers from New York and Boston and Philadelphia. The sons of the rich planters stopped often to talk about horse-racing, cock-fighting, and deer-stalking. But more than all else, these young fellows talked about the French war in the North.

One day they told of the dashing British officers who were stopping at Alexandria, and declared that red coats and gold lace were turning the heads of all the pretty girls.

Another day they said young Colonel George Washington, with a Virginia regiment, had joined the British General Forbes, and they were marching together to capture the French fort on the Ohio River.

And then, a few weeks later, they hurried in to tell how the French fort was taken, and how everybody thought that the French would be defeated at Quebec.

Now, all this talking was very exciting! Nobody enjoyed it more than Patrick himself. Yet talking would not settle bills. The tobacco crop failed a second time, and he was obliged to shut up his shop.

And so, at the age of twenty-three, Patrick Henry, with a wife and little children to provide for, did not have a shilling in his pocket. But his father helped a little and Sarah's father helped a little, and they managed to keep the wolf from the door.

"There is one thing I can say about Patrick," said Sarah's father; "he does not swear nor drink, nor keep bad company."

IV.—THE LICENSE TO PRACTICE LAW.

It was just about Christmas time that Patrick failed in business.

There was great merry-making in the neighborhood; and on Christmas eve, the young people were all invited to a party at the house of Colonel Dandridge, a rich planter living near the Henrys. Thomas Jefferson was one of the guests.

He was a fine lad, sixteen years old, and was on his way to attend William and Mary College at Williamsburg.

When Jefferson was introduced to Patrick Henry, he thought him a very rough-looking fellow; but he soon found that he was the best fiddler, the best story-teller, and the jolliest joker in the company.

When he heard about his misfortunes and saw the lonely little shop with its window boarded up and its door closed, he said to himself, "It is too bad that such a merry soul is so idle and shiftless!" He never expected to see the poor merchant again.

A few months later, as Jefferson was sitting in his room in Williamsburg, he heard a knock at the door.   Imagine his surprise when, upon opening it, he saw Patrick Henry, of Hanover County.

There he stood, dressed in coarse homespun and covered with the dust of his journey. His hair hung in tangles about his ears. He looked so shabby that the rich young student thought he had come to beg.

When Patrick told him he had come to the city to pass an examination to be a lawyer, Jefferson smiled and thought he must be joking. But the deep-set blue eyes looked very serious under the shaggy brow.

"I am going to try to make a man of myself, Tom," he said, "and if I pass with the judges I shall let you know."

A few days later Patrick called again. He was much elated as he showed his license to practice law in the courts of Virginia.

"I blundered through the questions with two of the judges," he said. "They signed my paper just to get rid of me, I think. When I went to the third judge, he refused at first even to ask me anything. He thought me a greenhorn; I am sure of it by the way he looked at me. But I showed

him that the others had signed for me, and then he
began to put questions.

"Of course, he asked me a great deal that I knew
nothing about. I was just thinking to myself that
he would soon quit in disgust, when he made a
statement that did not sound like good law. We
argued the question a long time. I got quite hot
over my side.

"At last Judge Randolph said, 'You defend
your opinion well, sir; but now let us look up the
law.' He opened one book and then another.
His face flushed. After a moment of silence he
exclaimed, 'Here are law books which you have
never read; yet you are right and I am wrong!
Mr. Henry, if your industry is only half equal to
your genius, you will prove an ornament to your
profession!'"

Jefferson himself expected to be examined some
day for the law, and listened eagerly to all that
Patrick said. And when he had finished, he gave
him his hand, and told him he wished him success,
and invited him for a walk through the city.

The two passed down the street together.

Now, Williamsburg was the capital of Virginia.

Here the governor lived and the House of Burgesses met to make the laws.

Just as the boys were admiring the governor's mansion, with its fine garden of roses, a great coach drawn by six milk-white horses drove out at the gate.

The governor sat inside the coach. He smiled, and waved his hand at young Thomas Jefferson, who doffed his three-cornered hat and bowed most gracefully.

Then many fair ladies smiled upon the rich and elegant college boy. No doubt, they wondered that he walked with such an awkward looking fellow; but Thomas Jefferson was pleased with the wit of his companion.

They walked through the park and then stopped at the famous Raleigh tavern, where Thomas told about the gay times the young folks had in the ball-room. " But nobody in Williamsburg plays the fiddle so well as you, Patrick," he said.

They visited the capitol, and went up the broad portico into the room where the burgesses met. And as they looked down from the lobby upon the empty seats below, Jefferson talked about the Virginia statesmen whom he had seen there at the last session.

He said that his favorite was Colonel George Washington, who had marched with Braddock against the Indians and had afterwards captured the French fort at the head of the Ohio.

It was all very interesting to Patrick. He wondered if he should ever meet the famous men who sat together on those benches and helped the king's officers make laws for the colony of Virginia. He was delighted with everything he saw, for he had never been in a town before.

At last he bade good bye to his courteous friend, and, mounting his horse, he rode away with his lawer's license safe in the saddle bags beneath him.

V.—THE KING AND HIS PROVINCE.

It was in 1760 when Patrick Henry got permission to be a lawyer. At that time Virginia, like most of the other colonies in America, was still a province belonging to England.

The king of England sent over a governor to

rule in his stead. The governor chose a few men
to advise him about the affairs of the province,
and when they met together they were called the
council.

The people elected delegates, called burgesses,
who met every year in Williamsburg with the
council. And when the burgesses and the council
agreed on any measure for the public good, it
became the law of the land.

Sometimes the king himself made laws for his
provinces, without asking the consent of anybody.
This did not please the people very well. Yet
they had always been loyal to their king, whatever
he did.

It was said that Virginia was the most loyal of
all the colonies. But when young George the
Third came to the throne, the Virginians had
hardly stopped shouting over his coronation before
they saw that he would make them a great deal
of trouble.

The first complaint was about the salaries of
the clergymen. Because there was so little coin
in the country, the people paid their debts in
paper money, or in tobacco.

The clergy had always been paid in tobacco; but one year, when the tobacco crop was poor, the law was passed that clergymen should be paid in paper money instead of tobacco. This made their salaries much smaller than ever before.

Now, some of the clergy in Virginia were noble men, and did a great deal of good, and among them was Patrick Henry's own uncle. But there were many who were not worthy of the name of clergymen.

They lived in fine houses. They went hunting with their hounds across country. They loved horse-racing, dice-playing, and wine. They courted the rich, and neglected the poor.

You can guess that such kind of men would not like to have their salaries made any less. They sent a petition to the king against it.

The king declared the law void; and then the clergymen went into court and sued the tax-collectors for the full amount of their pay.

Very few lawyers were willing to oppose the clergymen. The king was on their side, and the governor favored them, too.

But when some of the planters in Hanover County

asked young Patrick Henry to take a case against
the clergymen, he said he would do the best that
he could.

VI.—THE PARSONS' CAUSE.

When it was noised about that the "parsons"
were having a trial in the little brick court-house,
people hurried in on horse, on foot, and in car-
riages. There were rich planters in velvet and
lace, farmers in homespun, and poor whites in
rags.

As Patrick watched them from the door of the
tavern, he was glad that so many of his neighbors
would hear his speech. He knew that if he won
this case he would have many others.

But when he saw his uncle, the clergyman, step
from his carriage, his courage failed him. He
hastened to him, and said respectfully:

"Uncle, I am to try my first important case to-
day. I shall not be able to speak before you. I
would be too much embarrassed in your presence.
Besides, I shall be obliged to say some hard things
about the clergy."

"Well, Patrick, my boy," said his uncle kindly,
"it is not I who shall stand in the way of your success. I will go back home. But you would best
let the clergy alone. You will get the worst of
it."

And the good old man returned to the carriage,
and was driven away.

Then Patrick saw his father making his way
through the crowd. He had quite forgotten that
his father would be the judge at the trial. His
heart seemed to come into his throat. Yet there
was no help for him. The people were filling the
court-room, and the doorway, and all the windows.

He squeezed through the packed room. There,
in front, in a black robe, sat his father on a high
bench, and before him sat twenty clergymen in
one long row. And there were the twelve jurymen, who should bring in a verdict. It was a
great moment for the young lawyer.

When he arose to speak, he looked shabby and
awkward. His words came slowly. He hesitated
and almost stopped speaking. The planters hung
their heads. One whispered, "We should have

known better than to put the case in the hands of that shiftless fellow!"

The clergymen on the bench lifted their eyebrows, and winked and nodded to one another, as much as to say, "Our case is already won."

Judge Henry nearly sank from the bench in confusion at his son's poor speaking. "Ah, Patrick, Patrick," he thought, "you have failed on the farm and in the shop, and now you are going to fail at the law, and the wife and wee bairns at home will be wanting for food!"

But soon Patrick's voice became clear. The long, awkward body straightened up. The blue eyes flashed. He looked grand and majestic.

The crowds outside the windows, who had begun to laugh and talk, were silent. Those at the door leaned eagerly forward to see the speaker.

He told about the poverty of the people, and the taxes they had paid for the war with the French.

He dwelt on the failure of the tobacco crop, and on the struggles of the poor farmers to keep their families from starving.

Then he pictured how Christ had fed the poor,

and walked among the weak and the lowly of the earth.

And then, in scorn and anger, he pictured the many clergymen of Virginia who lived in fine houses, and feasted and drank while they were trying to take the last bit of bread from the tables of the poor.

His words were awful to the twenty clergymen. They shrank back in dismay.

Then the young lawyer stood like a lion at bay as he talked of the rights of the people.

He said the king of England had given the province of Virginia the right to make its own laws about the taxes. The House of Burgesses had passed a law providing for the use of paper instead of tobacco in payment of the clergy. This law, he said, was made to protect the poor from the oppressions of the rich.

His voice rang out clear and strong, and his eyes flashed strangely as he said that even a king had not the right to declare void a law made by the people.

" When a king becomes a tyrant," he cried, " he forfeits all right to obedience! "

Some who heard him looked frightened at such bold words. But as the speech went on, Patrick became more and more eloquent. He won the hearts of all. His father, the judge, forgot where he was, and tears streamed down his cheeks.

When the last words were uttered, the twelve jurymen went out. They soon brought back the verdict of one penny damages!

The clergymen had hoped to obtain several hundred dollars. They had lost their case, and they fled in anger and disappointment from the courtroom. But the planters shouted the name of their young lawyer. They bore him out on their shoulders and set him down in the yard where all might shake his hand.

And, for many years in Hanover County, if any one chanced to make a fine speech, the highest praise he could receive was that he was "almost equal to Patrick when he pleaded against the parsons."

VII.—THE STAMP ACT.

After his victory over the clergymen, Patrick Henry had all the business he could attend to.

Whoever got into trouble hastened to ask the young lawyer to help him get out of it.

His fees increased. He soon became so rich that he loaned money to his father, and then he loaned to Sarah's father.

He could not throw off his old habits at once. He still loved to hunt and to fish. Sometimes he was away in the forest whole days at a time.

Sometimes he came into the court-room with his gun in his hand and his buckskin clothes red with the blood of the deer he had killed. But he studied hard and read a great deal of history, and talked much with the people as he traveled about from court to court.

Now just at that very time there was good reason for talking. The king and his Parliament were beginning to make trouble. They saw the colonies getting richer and richer.

Ship after ship came over the sea laden with furs, wheat, tobacco, and rice from America. Even cotton was beginning to be profitable.

"Those colonies across the sea shall be taxed," said the king.

So Parliament, with the king's advice, made a

law that required all legal papers in America to be
stamped. If a man made a deed of his farm, or
wrote out a will on his death bed, or got a license
to marry, he had to use stamped paper bought in
England. The price to be paid for the paper was
much greater than the cost of it, and thus a large
tax might be collected.

The Americans said that they alone had the
right to vote a tax. They were willing to vote
for a tax, but Parliament should not do it for
them.

Almost all the colonies sent petitions to the king
against the Stamp Act. The province of Virginia
sent a petition signed by George Washington and
many others. But the king gave no answer.
What should be done ?

If the tax were paid once, it would have to be
paid twice.

" We must fight the law," said someone.

" But most of the burgesses are the mere tools of
the king," said another; " let us elect Patrick
Henry a burgess. He is bold and will defend our
rights."

And so it came about that Patrick Henry was

sent to the House of Burgesses to speak for the people of his county against the oppressions of the king and his Parliament.

VIII.—IN THE HOUSE OF BURGESSES.

It was a fine day in May when Patrick Henry came into Williamsburg to sit in the House of Burgesses.

No one paid the least attention to the young man in homespun as he rode along on his lean horse. There was too much else to think about.

The king had not listened to any petitions. The Stamp Act had become a law, and everybody on the streets was wondering what the burgesses would do.

When the House assembled, some of the burgesses said there should be nothing done until the other colonies were heard from.

Others said that, because the Stamp Act was now a law, it was best to obey it. And then the most of them sank back in their seats as if the question were settled.

But Patrick Henry rose to his feet. He looked very tall and awkward. He held in his hand the yellow leaf of an old law book, on which he had written some resolutions.

These resolutions declared that if a law was unjust it should be opposed; that the Virginians had a charter from the king granting the rights of English subjects; that English subjects had the right to tax themselves, and so the Virginians had that right; and that whoever claimed that Parliament could tax the Virginians without their consent was an enemy to the colony!

Those were very bold words to use about a law made by the king!

The most timid of the burgesses fairly trembled with fear as they listened.

Then Patrick Henry made a great speech. Nothing like it had ever been heard in Williamsburg.

It was all against the unjust tax, and he closed it with flashing eye, saying: "Cæsar had his Brutus, Charles the First his Cromwell, and George the Third"—

" Treason! treason!" shouted the friends of the
king.

" And George the Third," he repeated, " may
profit by their example—*If that be treason, make
the most of it!*" he cried in tones that echoed
through the hall.

Thomas Jefferson, the law student, who was
in the lobby, almost cheered aloud when he
heard the brave words.

George Washington, who sat with the burgesses,
nodded his head; and so many others believed
what Patrick Henry had said that the bold resolutions were adopted.

From that day Patrick Henry, the most eloquent man in Hanover County, was called the
most eloquent man in Virginia.

IX.—THE CONTINENTAL CONGRESS.

The Virginia resolutions against the Stamp
Tax were carried to the colonies in the North.
They were published in New England and
scattered all over the country.

The governor of Massachusetts wrote to the king's council: "I thought that the Americans would submit to the Stamp Act. But the Virginia resolves have proved an alarm bell."

And General Gage, the commander of the British forces, wrote from New York: "The Virginia resolves have given the signal for a general outcry all over the continent."

People now began to speak out more boldly. The Virginians declared they would not wear clothes bought in England until the tax was removed.

And when the rich planters went about clad in homespun, Patrick Henry looked quite as well as the best of them, and he talked much better than any.

After a time the king abolished the stamp tax, but he straightway put a tax on tea. Now, taxed tea was just as bad as taxed paper. People said they would not drink tea. And soon a swift courier rode into Williamsburg, saying that Boston had thrown the tea chests of the British merchants into the harbor.

Then another came in haste saying, that the king

had shut up the port of Boston. The British general would not even allow a little shallop to enter the bay, and he kept his soldiers standing in the streets of the city with their bayonets fixed.

When the House of Burgesses met and ordered a day of fasting and prayer for the trouble that had come upon Boston, Patrick Henry spoke more boldly than ever against the tyranny of the king.

Governor Dunmore ordered the burgesses to separate. They hurried to meet again at Raleigh Tavern. Here they appointed a committee to write to the other colonies about what should be done. There was much writing back and forth between the North and the South.

Many said there should be a convention to form a union of the colonies. But, in our forefathers' day, as in our own, there were some men who did not believe in experiments.

A member of the South Carolina legislature laughed at the idea of a convention: " What kind of a dish will a congress from the different British colonies make?" he said. " New England will throw in fish and onions, the Middle States flax-seed and flour, Maryland and Virginia will add tobacco, North Carolina pitch, tar, and turpentine, South Carolina rice and indigo, and Georgia will sprinkle the whole composition with sawdust. That is about the kind of a jumble you will make if you attempt a union between the thirteen British provinces."

But another member retorted: "I would not choose the gentleman who made these objections for my cook, but I venture to say that, if the colonies proceed to appoint deputies to a Continental Congress, they will prepare a dish fit to be presented to any crowned head in Europe."

At last the colonies agreed to choose delegates to meet in convention at Philadelphia.

The Virginians chose Peyton Randolph a delegate for his dignity, George Washington for his military knowledge, Richard Henry Lee and Patrick Henry for their eloquence, Edmund Pendleton for his knowledge of law, Richard Bland for his skill in writing, and Benjamin Harrison for his popularity with the planters.

And so we see that Patrick Henry was chosen with the richest men in Virginia to go to Philadelphia to attend the first Continental Congress.

The young lawyer was very busy for several weeks getting his affairs in order before starting on so long a journey.

X.—The Speech in Carpenters' Hall.

On a hot day in August, 1774, Patrick Henry and Edmund Pendleton set out for Philadelphia. They traveled on horseback over a bridle path through the forest, and swam all the streams.

At length they came to Mount Vernon, where Colonel Washington lived. Here they passed the night, and the following morning, after an early breakfast, Washington mounted his horse to go with them to Congress.

As the two guests, with their three-cornered hats in their hands, were bowing low to Martha Washington, she said, " I hope you will both stand firm. I know George will."

And you may be sure they started off more determined than ever to demand justice of the king.

They soon crossed the Potomac at the Falls, and then followed the path toward Baltimore. They were a noble group of men. Edmund Pendleton was much the oldest. His hair was gray and his face was earnest.

George Washington was in the prime of manhood. He sat his horse like a true cavalier, and in the uniform of a British colonel he looked like a soldier.

Patrick Henry was thirty-eight years old. The great orator stooped forward as he rode, and his clothes hung loosely about him. He was not very handsome, but when he spoke his face lighted up, and you would have said he was almost beautiful.

They talked very earnestly over the troubles with the king, and all three agreed that a crisis had come. They reached Philadelphia just in time for the convention; and so they did not become acquainted with many of the members from the other colonies before the meeting began.

After the delegates had assembled in a large brick building, called Carpenters' Hall, the roll was read and officers were elected. Then the place became very still. The delegates were almost all strangers to one another. Each feared to say anything lest he might offend some one else.

At last a member moved to open the convention with prayer. John Jay, of New York, hurried to oppose the motion. "No man," he said, "can expect Baptists, Presbyterians, Congregationalists, Episcopalians, Quakers, and Catholics to unite in worship."

But Samuel Adams, from "stiff-necked" Massachusetts, arose and said: "I, for my part, am no bigot. I can listen to a prayer from a gentleman of piety who is a patriot. I have heard that the reverend Mr. Duché, an Episcopalian, deserves that title; therefore, Mr. President, I move that Mr. Duché read prayers to-morrow morning."

The motion was carried. And then again the place became very still. Each man had the same complaints to make against the king, yet no one liked to speak of them.

The silence became so intense that some said afterwards they could hear their hearts beat.

At last a tall young man arose. Everybody turned about to look at him. He was dressed in dark grey homespun, his wig was unpowdered, and his sleeves had no frills.

He began very calmly to state why they had met together. But soon his voice swelled, his form became erect, his eyes glowed. All leaned forward to read his wonderful face. He closed with the words: "The distinctions between Virginians, Pennsylvanians, New Yorkers, and New Englanders are no more. I am not a Virginian, but an American!"

The delegates were amazed at his eloquence.

"Who is he? who is he?" they cried.

It was Patrick Henry, and from that day the best orator in Virginia was known as the best orator in America. He argued with the rest of the delegates not to import any more goods from England nor to export them to England until Parliament should respect the rights of Americans.

Henry spoke many times during the Congress; and when it was decided to appeal again to the king to allow the colonies to vote their own taxes, he was one of the committee chosen to write the petition.

Soon after this the first Continental Congress adjourned to meet when the king should send his reply.

XI.—Taking up Arms against the King.

When Henry reached home, the neighbors crowded around him, asking many questions about the city of Philadelphia and the people whom he had met there.

" Who was the greatest man there?" asked one.

" Always excepting yourself, Patrick," shouted another, laughing, " I'll warrant you were the greatest of all!"

Henry told them about the city that William Penn had built, and about the famous men who were at the congress.

There was Roger Sherman, of Connecticut, who "never said a foolish thing in his life." There was Samuel Adams, of Massachusetts, whose "head was wanted badly in England;" and his cousin John Adams, who " had forty towns in the Bay Colony at his back."

There was John Rutledge, of South Carolina, who was "by far the greatest orator of them all," with his brother Edward, who had learned fine manners at the court of the king, but had become a patriot while listening to the debates in Parliament on the tea tax.

There was Philip Livingston, of New York, whose letters to Edmund Burke had won that great English orator to the American cause; and there was John Jay, whose "pen was the finest in America."

"Of course, you know all about our own men," he said. "Everybody made much of Richard Henry Lee, for they had heard how he made a bonfire of the stamps; and Peyton Randolph was elected chairman of the convention. But for solid information and sound judgment," said Henry, "Colonel Washington was the greatest man in the Congress."

Now, the king gave no heed to the petition of Congress. He sent over a fleet of ships and an army to aid General Gage in making war on the colonies if they would not obey the law.

The second Virginia convention met in St. John's church, in Richmond, on the 2nd of March, 1775.

Patrick Henry moved in a convention that Virginia be put in a state of defence.

Many opposed doing this. They said it was the duty of every man to obey the king.

And so the Virginians were divided in opinion. Those who were loyal to the king were called

St John's Church.

Red Hill.

The Hanover Court-House.

tories, and those who refused to obey his unjust laws were called whigs.

Patrick Henry, George Washington, Thomas Jefferson, Richard Henry Lee, and many others were whigs ; but there were also many powerful men who were tories. When the tories opposed the motion to defend the colony, Patrick Henry made a wonderful speech.

"We must fight," he said. "An appeal to arms and to the God of Hosts is all that is left us. They tell us, sir, that we are weak! But when shall we be stronger? Will it be the next week or the next year? Will it be when a British guard shall be stationed in every house?

"Sir, we are not weak. Three millions of people armed in the holy cause of liberty, and in such a country as that which we possess, are invincible by any force which our enemy can send against us.

"Besides, sir, we shall not fight our battles alone. There is a just God who presides over the destinies of nations, and who will raise up friends to fight our battles for us.

"Gentlemen, we may cry peace! peace! but there is no peace. The next gale that sweeps from the

north will bring to our ears the clash of resounding
arms. Our brethren in Boston are already in the
field. Why stand we here idle?

"Is life so dear, or peace so sweet, as to be purchased at the price of chains and slavery? Forbid
it, Almighty God! I know not what course others
may take, but, as for me, give me liberty or give
me death!"

The faces of all were pale. The tories were
quaking with fear at the thought of having taken
part in such a meeting.

But Lee and Jefferson spoke in favor of arming
the colony, and Washington nodded his head,
though he said nothing.

In the end it was voted to take up arms against
the king's troops.

Meanwhile, the battles of Concord and Lexington were fought, near Boston. About the same
time Governor Dunmore seized the powder at
Williamsburg and sent it on board a British ship.

The whigs armed themselves. They rallied
about Patrick Henry, and set out for Williamsburg to demand the powder.

Tories along the march begged Henry not to

plunge the colony into a war with the governor. But he pushed on his way, and the whigs joined the ranks, until over five hundred were in line.

Governor Dunmore fled from the city. Very soon after, however, he sent a promise to pay for the powder he had carried away.

Then Patrick Henry disbanded the army and started for Philadelphia to attend the second Continental Congress. His friends, fearing the governor might have him arrested, mounted their horses and rode with him to the Potomac River. As he was ferried across to the Maryland side, they gave cheer after cheer and wished him success on his journey.

XII.—The Declaration of Independence.

When Henry arrived at Philadelphia, the Congress was already in session.

One of the new delegates was Benjamin Franklin, of Pennsylvania, who had just returned from London and knew all about the king and his Parliament.

Another new delegate was John Hancock, of

Massachusetts, who told of the battles of Concord and Lexington.

The very day that Henry took his seat news came from the north that Colonel Ethan Allen had captured Ticonderoga, on Lake Champlain, with a large amount of arms and ammunition.

It was decided that the colonies must be put in a state of defence.

There was much to be done. Ships were to be built, cities on the coast to be fortified, treaties made with the Indians, and more appeals sent in to the king. It was agreed to raise troops from all the colonies, and George Washington was made commander-in-chief of the colonial army.

Patrick Henry was glad that his friend had been honored with such a high office.

Yet he knew that it was a great risk to head a rebellion against the king.

Washington knew this, too. He wanted to be loyal to the king, but he felt he must fight for the rights belonging to all English subjects.

His eyes were full of tears as he clasped Henry by the hand and said: "I fear this day will begin the decline of my reputation."

He soon left Philadelphia to take command of the American troops at Cambridge.

When Congress was adjourned, Henry and the other delegates from Virginia returned home to meet in a convention.

The governor had fled to a British ship, and so a committee was appointed to rule in his stead. Then it was decided to raise troops in the colony, and Patrick Henry was made commander-in-chief.

Soldiers hurried from every county in Virginia to the camping ground at Williamsburg. There were trappers in buckskin, and hunters in green shirts, and rich planters in fine uniforms. There was the sound of fife and drum, and banners were seen everywhere. Governor Dunmore called the whigs rebels, and summoned tories, negroes, and Spaniards to fight them.

But before the troops came to battle, Patrick Henry resigned command. He was needed in the colonial convention at Williamsburg.

The convention met on the 6th of May, 1776.

Among the new delegates was James Madison. He was just twenty-five years old. He was a great scholar, but he was so shy that he did not attract much attention in his first debate.

Another new delegate was Edmund Randolph. He was twenty-three years old. His father was a tory, and had sailed away to England, but young Randolph remained in America to help fight for liberty.

James Madison and Edmund Randolph listened with delight to Patrick Henry's speeches.

They said he seemed like a pillar of fire, which was leading the convention through the night of despair.

When the orator proposed that the colonies should declare themselves free from Great Britain, most of the delegates were convinced that this was the only thing to do.

And so, on the 15th of May, the Virginians resolved to instruct their delegates in Congress at Philadelphia to propose a declaration of independence.

The British flag was taken down from the staff on the capitol, and a Continental flag was hoisted with thirteen bars for the thirteen colonies.

Then Patrick Henry and some others wrote out a constitution for the state of Virginia.

You know that every state in these days has a written constitution, but in those days most of the states had charters granted by the king.

It was agreed that Virginia should have a Senate and a House of Representatives to make the laws which the people wanted, a governor who should enforce the laws, and judges who should preside in the courts.

The constitution of Virginia seemed so wise that it became a model for the other states.

On June 7th, Richard Henry Lee, one of the Virginia delegates, offered the resolution in Congress that the "United Colonies are, and of right ought to be, free and independent states."

Thomas Jefferson wrote the *Declaration of Independence*, and after a long debate it was signed on the 4th of July, 1776.

And when the news reached Williamsburg, bells rang, bonfires blazed in the streets, and powder sizzed and spluttered in the gutters. It was the very first Fourth of July celebration in Virginia.

XIII.—THE FIRST GOVERNOR OF THE STATE OF VIRGINIA.

The Declaration of Independence was read from the steps of the governor's mansion at Williamsburg. Now, who do you think was governor? It was Patrick Henry. He had been elected before the news of the great event had reached Virginia. There he was in the mansion of the king's governors. He had won the first place in the state by his own merit.

His father and his wife, who had helped him in all the struggles on the farm and in the shop, were dead. But his aged mother, whom he loved very tenderly, was living to see his success.

George Washington and Thomas Jefferson and other whig friends wrote him beautiful letters of greeting in his new office.

But the tories laughed when they heard that Patrick Henry was elected governor. "A pretty governor he will make," they said, "with his buckskin breeches and homespun coat!"

But Governor Henry wished to represent the people as well as Lord Dunmore had represented the king. He wore a powdered wig and black velvet clothes, and long silk hose, and shoes with silver buckles, and in cold weather he wore an ample scarlet coat.

He did not walk the streets with his dog and gun any more, but rode in a carriage drawn by four horses, and saluted the people as gracefully as the king's governors had done. The people were very proud of their governor, and he was so kind and gentle that everybody loved him.

After a time he married the beautiful granddaughter of Alexander Spotswood, who had once been the king's governor of Virginia. This made the rich planters respect him more than ever.

There was much for Governor Henry to do. The tories were plotting mischief in the state, and the war in the North was raging.

General Washington wrote again and again to Governor Henry, asking him to send more men and more supplies, and he always sent them when he could.

In October, 1777, when the British General Burgoyne surrendered to the American army at Saratoga, New York, he said the Virginia regiment was the finest in the world.

But about that very time Washington, the pride of all the regiments, was defeated on the Brandywine, in Delaware. No one grieved over this misfortune more than Governor Henry. He hurried to send food and clothing to Washington's army.

Then he sent George Rogers Clark with a regiment to the far West to capture the forts held by the British north of the Ohio River. The Indians were awed and the forts were taken from the British.

If this expedition had failed, the country which makes the states of Ohio, Indiana, Illinois, Wisconsin, Michigan, and a part of Minnesota might to-day belong to Canada. And so these states have much for which to remember Patrick Henry.

Now, according to law, a governor might only be elected three times in succession. When Henry's third term had expired, Thomas Jefferson was elected governor, and the great orator retired to his estate among the Blue Ridge Mountains.

XIV.—THE CLOSE OF THE WAR.

It is quite certain that Patrick Henry would have strapped on his knapsack to fight for his country if he had not been needed to help make the laws. He was elected to the legislature to help provide means to carry on the war.

The British armies had failed in the North. So they came marching into Virginia to capture the South. They burned and plundered the towns on the coast. The people fled to the mountains.

The legislature kept moving from one place to another for safety.

One day the British General Tarleton was hurrying with his troopers to arrest the lawmakers. A Virginian captain, who saw him from the window of a tavern, mounted his horse and rode by the shortest way to Charlottesville. He burst into the room where the legislature sat, crying, "Tarleton is coming!"

There was a rush for three-cornered hats. The lawmakers decided, as they ran, to meet at Staunton, beyond the mountains.

They mounted their horses and fled in different directions.

It is said that as Patrick Henry, Benjamin Harrison, Judge Tyler, and Colonel Christian were

hurrying along, they saw a little hut in the forest.
An old woman was chopping wood by the door.
The men were very hungry, and stopped to ask
her for food.

"Who are you?" she asked.

"We are members of the legislature," said
Patrick Henry; "we have just been compelled to
leave Charlottesville on account of the British."

"Ride on, then, ye cowardly knaves!" she said
in wrath. "Here are my husband and sons just
gone to Charlottesville to fight for ye, and you
running away with all your might. Clear out!
Ye shall have nothing here."

"But," replied Mr. Henry, "we were obliged
to flee. It would not do for the legislature to be
broken up by the enemy. Here is Mr. Benjamin
Harrison; you don't think he would have fled had
it not been necessary?"

"I always thought a great deal of Mr. Harrison
till now," answered the old woman, "but he'd
no business to run from the enemy." And she
started to shut the door in their faces.

"Wait a moment, my good woman," cried Mr.
Henry; "would you believe that Judge Tyler

or Colonel Christian would take to flight if there
were not good cause for so doing?"

" No, indeed, that I wouldn't."

" But," he said, " Judge Tyler and Colonel Christian are here."

" They are? Well, I would never have thought
it. I didn't suppose they would ever run away
from the British; but since they have, they shall
have nothing to eat in my house. You may ride
along."

Things were getting desperate. Then Judge
Tyler stepped forward: " What would you say, my
good woman, if I were to tell you that Patrick
Henry fled with the rest of us?"

" Patrick Henry!" she answered angrily, " I
should tell you there wasn't a word of truth in
it! Patrick Henry would never do such a cowardly thing."

" But this is Patrick Henry," said Judge Tyler.

The old woman was astonished; but she stam-
mered and pulled at her apron string, and said:
'' Well, if that's Patrick Henry, it must be all
right. Come in, and ye shall have the best I have
in the house." Even this ignorant woman in

the woods had heard of the courage and patriotism of Patrick Henry.

The legislature met again at last, and took measures to collect soldiers and supply food, clothing, and arms to fight the British.

The next year Washington himself came down from New York, and a French fleet, sent over by King Louis the Sixteenth of France, entered Chesapeake Bay. Lord Cornwallis, the British general, was hemmed in on all sides. He surrendered his army; and soon the British soldiers and many tories sailed away and left the American colonies to govern themselves.

Three years later General Washington and Marquis de Lafayette visited Virginia. The state wished to do great honor to the commander-in-chief of the American armies and to the young French nobleman, who had fought for liberty. And so Patrick Henry was chosen to make a speech of welcome.

The French general did not understand the English language very well; but when he saw the glowing eyes and the speaking face, and heard the rich tones of the orator's voice, he said Mr. Henry was a wonderful man.

XV.—The Constitution of the United States.

The very next day after this great speech of welcome to Washington and Lafayette, Patrick Henry became governor of Virginia again. There were many grave questions to be solved. What should be done with the tories? That was one of the questions.

"Tar and feather them!" cried some.

"Welcome them and all other subjects of Great Britain," cried Governor Henry. "The tories were mistaken, but the quarrel is over. We have peace again. Let us lay aside prejudice. These people who sided with the king are intelligent and industrious. We need men and women to help make a strong nation. Let all come who will."

When some wanted to keep English ships out of the harbors, that the French and other friendly nations might trade more with us, Governor Henry said: "No! Why should we fetter commerce? Let her be free as the air, and she will return on the wings of the four winds of heaven to bless our land with plenty."

Thus the great man pleaded liberty for all.

After serving faithfully for two years as governor, he began again to practice law in the courts.

The soldiers of the Revolution had been paid in promises on paper by the Continental Congress. They needed money so badly that they could not wait for Congress to pay, and sold the promises at low prices to speculators.

When Patrick Henry favored the passage of a bill in the legislature to prevent the sale of the paper at such low prices, one of the speculators was so influenced by his eloquence that he exclaimed, "That bill ought to pass!" although its passage would spoil his own profits.

Now, since the war with England was over, it was clearly seen that the United States of America could not make a good government without a more permanent union. There was no president. Congress was disbanding. Soon there would be no government at all.

The colonies agreed to hold a convention at Philadelphia to revise the Articles of Confederation which had kept them together during the war.

Patrick Henry was appointed a delegate, with George Washington, James Madison, and others;

but his health was too poor for him to take the long journey.

The convention at Philadelphia adopted the Constitution of the United States as we have it to-day, without the amendments.

Eight States soon agreed to the Constitution. Would Virginia ratify it? Everybody said that New York and the rest of the states would act with Virginia.

General Washington sent Patrick Henry a copy of the Constitution, and urged him to persuade the people to adopt it.

Now, we have seen that, when the king was oppressing the colonies with taxes, Patrick Henry was one of the first to propose a union. But he thought the new plan of government gave too much power to Congress and the president. He said there should be amendments to the Constitution, so that the states might have more freedom.

No one had ever known a government without a king, and it was very difficult to suit everybody.

There was a long debate in a convention at Richmond. All the other colonies watched eagerly to see if Virginia would agree to the new plan of union. Mr. Henry urged the amendments.

At last the Constitution of the United States was ratified by Virginia, with the recommendation that amendments should be adopted when they seemed necessary. And some of the very amendments proposed by Patrick Henry were afterwards adopted by Congress.

To-day the Constitution has fifteen amendments, which have helped to make our government the best in the world.

XVI.—"THE SUN HAS SET IN ALL HIS GLORY."

After the Constitutional Convention at Richmond, Patrick Henry continued to practice law in the courts.

He rode from place to place on horseback or in an old gig; and at the taverns where he stopped he was always surrounded by an admiring crowd.

Wealth came. He bought many plantations and prospered greatly.

Then, as the years bent his shoulders and

wrinkled his high brow, he retired to the quiet of
an estate, called Red Hill, on the Staunton River.

The hospitable house stood on a slight rise of
ground, surrounded by groves of oak, pine, and
walnut trees.

Below it stretched the green valley, with its
winding stream and gently sloping hills. In the
distance towered the lofty peaks of the Blue
Ridge.

In full view of this beautiful scene, the noble
man sat often in a great armchair under the shade
of a spreading walnut tree, or walked from grove
to grove as he talked with himself. No one inter-
rupted him then; but when the hour of solitude was
over his grandchildren gathered around with a
shout.

There were frolics on the grass, where the silver-
haired grandfather was the noisiest of the merry-
makers. And he often told stories, while the little
ones listened with breathless attention, or he made
his violin mimic the birds, while the joyous band
about him vied at guessing which songster was a
prisoner in the instrument.

Nothing tempted the great orator from this

delightful retreat of his old age.   Virginia elected
him governor for a sixth term, but he firmly
refused the honor.   His friend Washington, who
had become President of the United States, asked
him to be Minister to Spain, and then he asked him
to be Secretary of State, and then to be Chief
Justice of the Supreme Court ; but he would
listen to no offers of high place.

When John Adams became President, he urged
Mr. Henry to go as an envoy to France, but he
refused.   The years lay heavy on his shoulders
because of ill-health.   Besides, he had won laurels
enough.

In January, 1799, a letter came from Mount Vernon, marked " *Confidential.*"   It was in the hand-
writing of George Washington.

Just at this time several states claimed the right
to declare void some laws made by Congress.   The
laws were not wise, and many in Virginia said it
was the duty of the legislature to refuse to obey
them.

Washington implored Patrick Henry to speak in
defence of the government of the United States.

Now, the great orator did not like the laws very

well himself; but he said, when an Act of Congress became a law, it was the duty of every citizen to obey it. He agreed to tell the people what he thought about it.

It had been many years since Patrick Henry had spoken in public; and when it was noised around that he would speak at Charlottesville court-house, people flocked in from all over the country to hear him.

The college in the next county closed for a holiday, and president, professors and students hurried to find standing room in the court-house.

Before the hour for the meeting, such crowds followed the orator about that a clergyman said, to rebuke them: "Mr. Henry is not a god!"

"No," said Mr. Henry, who was deeply moved because the people were so devoted to him; "no, indeed, my friends, I am but a poor worm of the dust."

When the great orator arose to speak, he seemed stooped with age. His face was pale and careworn.

At first his voice was cracked and shrill, and his gestures were feeble; but soon his bowed

head became erect, his blue eyes glowed, his
features looked like those of a young man, his
voice rang out like music to the farthest listener
of the thousands standing in the courtyard.

He told them they had planted thorns in his
pillow, and that he could not sleep while Virginia
was a rebel to the government of the United
States. The Virginians had dared to pronounce
the laws of Congress without force. Only the
Supreme Court of the United States had the right
to do that.

He said they would drive the United States
government to arms against them to enforce her
rightful authority; and, because they were too
weak alone, the Virginians would call in the Spaniards, or the French, or the English, from over
the sea, to help them fight against the government
of the United States, and then these foreign
powers would make them slaves.

He asked if Charlotte County had the right to
defy the laws of Virginia. Then he showed them
how Virginia belonged to the United States, just
as Charlotte County belonged to Virginia.

" Let us preserve our strength united," he said,

"against whatever foreign nation may dare to enter our territory."

The vast multitude hung on each word and look. When he had finished his magnificent speech, he was very weak; and as he was carried into the tavern near by, some one said, " The sun has set in all his glory."

He returned to his home. A few weeks later, while sitting in his chair, he died.

Just before the end came, he prayed aloud in a clear voice for his family and for his country. When he breathed for the last time, his old family physician left his side to throw himself down under the trees and sob aloud. And everybody who had known the brave, generous, and gifted Patrick Henry grieved over his loss. ·

A marble slab covers his grave, inscribed with the name, the birth, and the death, and the words: " His fame is his best epitaph."

Before the year closed, George Washington died also, and there was mourning throughout the land for these two great patriots, who had done so much for Virginia and for the young republic of the United States.

THE STORY OF
ALEXANDER HAMILTON

THE STORY OF ALEXANDER HAMILTON.

I.—THE ORPHAN BOY OF NEVIS.

In the British West Indies there is a little island called Nevis. The cliffs along its coast are high, and the waves beat against them day and night.

A hundred and fifty years ago there were more French than English people in Nevis; but the English were hurrying as fast as they could to occupy the island, because it was so fertile and was such a fine shipping station.

Among the merchants who went there to try their fortunes was James Hamilton. He was a Scotchman by birth. His people were distinguished, and he himself was a generous and agreeable gentleman.

Everybody liked James Hamilton; he prospered greatly in his new home, and married a beautiful French lady, and they had several children. Then the children died, one by one, until all were gone except the youngest son.

This boy was born on January 11, 1757, and he was named Alexander, after his grandfather in Scotland. He was a winsome baby; he had fine linen and silken garments, and it was said that he had an easy life before him.

Very soon, however, Alexander's father lost all his money, and could hardly keep his family from starving; but the beautiful French mother was always cheerful and gay, and tried to make the child happy. She took long walks with him in the sunshine; and when his little legs were tired with tramping over the sand, she sat down by him on the white beach and told him stories in her own French language.

One day this loving mother became very ill; then she died, and Alexander saw her carried away and buried by the side of his little brothers and sisters; but he never forgot his mother, nor the language she taught him to speak.

When he first went to school, he was so small that he stood on the table by the side of his teacher while learning the Ten Commandments. He did not go to school very long, because his father had no money to pay for his teaching.

When he was only twelve years old, he was sent to the island of Santa Cruz to clerk in the counting-house of Mr. Nicholas Cruger. There were rows of desks in the counting-house where clerks were busy writing, and iron chests where money was kept, and scales where workmen weighed bags of sugar, boxes of indigo, and bales of cotton ; and outside the wide doors stood carts and wheelbarrows to carry the merchandise to the waiting ships in the harbor.

Alexander was very busy in the counting-house. He wrote down the long lists of goods for the ladings, and the dates when the ships sailed, and when they came back to port again. His master, Mr. Cruger, was a thrifty merchant. " Method is the soul of business," he often said, as he bustled about the counting-room.

Alexander did not like clerking very well ; he wrote to a young friend in Nevis : " I would willingly risk my life, though not my character, to exalt my station."

Those were brave words for a boy of twelve years, were they not? He would not risk his character to improve his fortune!

I think you will find that Alexander Hamilton always prized his character more than life itself.

Now, although he did not like his work, he did not shirk it. He was so diligent that, when only fourteen years old, he was left in charge of the counting-office while his employer was absent in Boston.

He was small for his age ; he must have looked like a child playing at keeping store as he went about with a quill pen over one ear, taking note of what the other clerks did. Some letters still exist which he sent to Boston, telling how the business was getting along ; they are neat and exact ; they must have pleased his employer very much.

When the duties of the day were over, Alexander studied in books which he borrowed from his friend, the Rev. Mr. Knox. He was fond of arithmetic and history, and he liked to read the lives of the great men who have helped to make the world better and happier.

Now, just about this time, a hurricane swept down upon the Leeward Islands ; ships were tossed upon the rocks by the wind, trees were torn from their roots, and villages were lifted up and thrown into the raging sea. It was all so terrible that the bravest men fled in terror into the caves ; but Alexander was not afraid; he watched the storm from a high ledge of rocks, and he thought it was so grand that everybody should know just how it looked; so he wrote all about it, and sent the account to a newspaper.

When people read it, they were astonished at the language. The description of the hurricane was so beautiful that many who had hidden in the caves wished they had stayed in the open to watch it.

Who on the island could write so well? Nobody knew. The governor set to work to find out ; and when he learned that the pale little clerk in the counting-house was the author, he said that such a bright boy should have an education.

ᐧ Now, people were so eager to contribute money for this that Alexander soon had enough to pay his expenses at school for several years ; then, because there were no good schools in the island, it was decided to send him to one of the large cities in America.

And so, clad in a new suit of clothes, Alexander

Hamilton climbed the gang plank of a British packet bound for Boston. The sailors shouted; the ropes were drawn up; there were hands waving farewell, and soon the tall cliffs of the island were lost in the mists of the sea.

II.—The Voyage.

When the vessel had left the land behind, Alexander began to look about him. He soon knew the sailors by name, and they all grew very fond of him. His best friend was a Scotch pilot who had been in service for many years. This old pilot told Alexander how King George of England had sent armies across the sea to help the Americans fight the French.

"Those Frenchmen wanted the earth," he said. "They first wanted the coast of Maine, and then they wanted the beaver lands on the great river called the Ohio. And never a bit would they let the British trade for the furs of the Injuns. Every man knows that the land belonged to the king; and his majesty sent over the pick of his armies to fight for it."

Then he told how the French forts on the Ohio had been taken by the British General Forbes and a "likely American lad" by the name of George Washington, and how the forts along the St. Lawrence had been seized by the brave General Wolfe and his army; and how, at last, the British had gained the great fresh water lakes in the north, and all the land along the Ohio.

The old man had his own ideas about the people who lived in the colonies

"I cannot well make out these Americans," he said. "They're a headstrong lot, laddie. They've made trouble from the first; and, now they've had a hand fighting the French, they're pesky ready to fall upon the king's troops sent over to keep them in order."

And while the old tar pulled away at his wheel, he told how the Americans would not consent to be taxed by Parliament; how Patrick Henry, a bold young man in Virginia, had defied the king in open meeting about a stamp tax, and how Boston and other cities had refused to buy any more goods from British merchants till the tax was taken off.

"It makes bad shipping business, laddie," he groaned; "and it's all bad from the beginning of it, and I know you'll say so yourself when you see the carryings on.

"They call themselves 'Sons of Liberty,' and have big meetings on the green, and they do a power of speaking and reading newspapers instead of smoking their pipes and keeping the peace.

"Last year, at Boston, when the king's troops stood in the streets to keep the rascals quiet, the folk came and hooted at them, and would not go home; and the troops fired the guns, and killed two or three of the men.

"And Samuel Adams, a very bold man, with the whole town at his back, ordered the king's troops out of Boston. Think of that, laddie !

"The king's officers wanted orders from the king before they put the bayonets to the throats of the villains; so they took the troops to an island in the harbor; and there they are to-day, keeping close watch on the town. I think we'll see their bayonets shining when we sail up the bay."

Alexander made up his mind that the Americans must be very wicked indeed. On the island

of Nevis, no one said a word against the great
king of England who sat on a throne.

Alexander learned all he could about the Americans. He was almost afraid to go to a country
where men were bold enough to defy King
George's grenadiers.

The ship plunged slowly along towards his new
home.

One night he heard the cry of "Fire! fire!" He
ran to the hatchway. The deck was in a red glare
of light. The sailors were running to and fro with
buckets of water. Everybody thought the vessel
would be destroyed, but at last the fire was put out.

A few days later, the ship passed an island
where long lines of soldiers in red coats were
marching. The bayonets gleamed in the sunshine, and the voices of the captains rang over
the water as they gave their commands.

"There they are, sure enough, laddie," said the
old Scotch pilot. "The king's troops are waiting,
and watching the town of Boston!"

And when Alexander saw the steeples of the
city, he wondered if the king's troops would ever
march again into Boston with their bayonets fixed.

III.—"THE LITTLE WEST INDIAN."

Alexander Hamilton landed at Boston on a bright day in October, 1772. He had only time to look about the docks. Then he took a packet for New York, where he intended to go to school.

When he reached New York, he hunted up some clergymen, to whom he gave letters from his friend, Mr. Knox. These gentlemen received him with much kindness, and advised him to go to the grammar school at Elizabethtown, in New Jersey.

Before very long, Alexander was hard at work. He soon had many friends in Elizabethtown. Governor Livingston welcomed him to his home, and he often spent his evenings reading in the governor's library.

Once, when the baby of a lady friend died, he watched all night by the little casket. The room was lighted dimly with one candle, and as he sat alone such beautiful thoughts came to him about the dead child that he wrote them out in verse. The next morning he gave the verses to the sad mother. They comforted her very much.

At the end of one year, Alexander had been so

diligent in the grammar school that he was ready for college. He went to see the president of Princeton College. He told him he was anxious to finish his studies as soon as possible, and asked to be allowed to double the work outside of the class.

The president declared that no such thing had ever been done, but promised to talk with the officers about it. He soon wrote Alexander that it had been decided to refuse his request. "But I am convinced," he said, "that you will do honor to any seminary in which you may be educated."

Alexander returned to New York. He entered Columbia College, which was then called King's College. Here he was so witty and amiable that he made many friends. He wrote a play, which the British officers acted, and he joined a debating club where the students talked much about the troubles with the king.

Alexander remembered what the old Scotch pilot had said about the Americans, and at first he always debated on the king's side.

But one time, I do not know why, he went up to Boston. Perhaps it was to attend to some business for his old employer at the counting-house. He found Boston in great excitement. A few nights before, the people in that city had met together to talk about the tax which Parliament had put on tea. They said they would not buy taxed tea, and that the ships in the harbor must take it back to England; but the king's governor would not send the tea back. Then some of the men dressed themselves like Indians, and hurried down to the harbor. They climbed up the sides of the ships and threw the tea overboard.

Now, the people knew very well that they would be punished for this bold act. Every night they held great public meetings. You may be sure that Alexander Hamilton attended all the meetings while he was in Boston.

He heard Samuel Adams, John Hancock, James Otis, and other patriots speak.

They said they were willing to pay taxes if they might vote like the freemen of England; but not a single American was allowed to sit in Parliament, and so Parliament had no right to tax Americans.

They said, if one tax were paid, many more must be paid; and, if the people dared to resist the law of Parliament, British troops would soon be placed in every town.

They said they were willing to obey a king, but they would not obey a tyrant.

The more Alexander listened to the talks of these great men, the more he admired them. He even found himself clapping his hands and cheering with all the rest when they cried, "No taxation without representation!"

And when he returned to New York, he would not defend the king's laws any more. He argued in debate on the side of the patriots.

He often walked under the shade of a grove of trees, talking low to himself. And when the neighbors passed by, they pointed him out and said, "There is the little West Indian, who makes such fine speeches in King's College."

IV.—"THE VINDICATOR OF CONGRESS."

Not long after young Hamilton's return to New York, news came that the king and his council

had closed the port of Boston. British soldiers
had marched into the city with bayonets fixed.
They would not allow an American vessel in the
harbor, not even a fishing smack.

The trade of the merchants was ruined. More
than half the people were without work, and hundreds would starve if food were not sent overland
from the other towns on the coast.

There was great excitement in New York over
this news from Boston. On a hot afternoon in
July a crowd of people met on the green to talk
about it.

Many spoke; but a slender boy, who sat listening, thought they had left out some very important
arguments. He stepped to the front. His face
was pale. He was so small that he looked like a
child; yet his voice rang out clear and strong, and
he spoke with so much elegance that people were
amazed. "Who is he?" they asked. It was
Alexander Hamilton, only seventeen years old.
"Ah, the wee lad," said one; "he is bigger than
he looks!"

The excitement about the taxes continued until
all the colonies agreed to meet in a convention at

Philadelphia. This convention was called the Continental Congress. The delegates decided to resist the taxes to the bitter end.

Then the people were divided into two parties. Those who were willing to obey the king's unjust demands were called tories, and those who refused to obey them were called whigs.

And whigs and tories were talking from morning till night. Some New York merchants met together at the coffee-house to consider their condition.

They said that all they had was on the sea. Prosperity depended on trade, and the Continental Congress at Philadelphia must not hurt trade with England by opposing the king's laws too much. They said that everybody must be cautious.

Now, Alexander Hamilton was at this meeting. He felt that to keep up trade at the expense of liberty would destroy trade in the end, and he decided to tell the merchants what he thought.

He mounted a chair. Smiles were seen about the room. Someone said: "What brings that child here? The poor boy will disgrace himself."

But the two years in the counting-house had taught the little West Indian more about British trade than most of the merchants knew. He made one of the very best speeches of the evening. He urged sympathy with Congress, and so pleased the rich men that they shook hands with him. They said he would be a great man some day.

Now, Dr. Cooper, the president of Columbia College, was a tory, and wrote a letter in a newspaper against the Continental Congress.

Alexander Hamilton replied to Dr. Cooper with much wit. He signed his letter, "A Sincere Friend to America." The letter was well written. Everybody wanted to read it. The demand for the newspaper was so great that the printer could not publish it fast enough. "Who *is* this 'Sincere Friend to America'?" men asked on the streets.

Some said it was Governor Livingston. Others said that only John Jay, the eloquent lawyer, could have written such a fine letter. Dr. Cooper said it *must* be John Jay, and he was so angry about it that he would not speak to him on the streets.

And all the time young Hamilton was laughing to himself about their bad guessing!

Some collegians had seen the letter before it was published, and told, at last, who the "Sincere Friend to America" was. Then people admired the "Little West Indian" more than ever. They said he would some day be an honor to New York, and they called him the "Vindicator of Congress."

V.—"The Little Lion."

Not long after that, a battle was fought at Lexington, near Boston.

Everybody saw that there must be a war. Congress called on all the colonies for volunteers, and appointed George Washington commander-in-chief of the American army. General Washington soon drove the British out of Boston, and hurried away to prevent them from taking New York.

Then King George sent over a great fleet with cannon and armed men. Some of the men were Hessians. They could not speak a word of English, yet they were hired by the king to fight his English subjects. This made the Americans more angry than ever. They said that a king who would do such a thing as that was not worthy of obe-

dience, and that the colonies should not be a
part of England any more. The Continental
Congress signed the *Declaration of Independence*,
and then war with England began in real
earnest.

Meanwhile, Alexander Hamilton was studying
how to build forts and drill soldiers. When it
was known that the British fleet was coming against
New York, he joined a company of volunteers.
They called themselves " Hearts of Oak," and
made a very brave showing indeed in their
green uniforms and leather caps, with " Freedom
or Death " on the bands.

It became necessary to remove some cannon from
the battery. The " Hearts of Oak " agreed to do
it. As they stood on the shore, pulling and tug-
ging at a heavy gun, the British fired at them from
the ships. A comrade fell dead at Hamilton s side;
but the young men stood their ground, and the
gun was at last removed to safety.

Now, when the people in the city heard this
firing from the British ships, they rushed into the
streets, crying: " Down with the tories !" " Down
with the hirelings of the king !" And one of the

first men they wanted to hang was Dr. Cooper, the president of Columbia College.

You remember that this was the tory whom Hamilton had opposed in the newspapers. Yet Hamilton knew that it would be a wicked thing to seize a defenseless man.

He was tired and heated from his work with the gun; but when he saw the angry mob surging toward the president's house, he hurried to it by a short street, and stood on the steps.

He told the people they were bringing disgrace on the name of liberty. He thought he would keep on talking in a very loud voice until the president might escape by a back door.

Dr. Cooper could not believe that Hamilton was generous enough to defend him. He thought he was down there on the front steps inciting the mob to burn his house. So he looked out of the window and called: "Don't listen to him, gentlemen; he's crazy! he's crazy!"

At last, the old scholar learned the truth, and escaped through a back door to a British man-of-war which lay in the harbor.

At another time, while the mobs were rushing to

destroy the printing presses of the tories, Hamilton again interfered.   He said the rights of all citizens should be protected, and begged the frantic
men to respect the law.

Soon after this, Hamilton was made captain of
an artillery company.

He was very proud of his company.   He spent
all his money to equip his men, and trained them
until they were the best soldiers in New York.

One day, as they were at drill, loading and un-
loading the big guns, taking them apart, putting
them together again, and running with them back
and forth, who should pass but Washington himself!   The great general stopped at the drill
ground to watch the artillery company.

He was so pleased with the bright face and the
commanding tones of the little captain that he
asked who he was; and then he slowly passed on,
repeating to himself: "Alexander Hamilton, the
'Vindicator of Congress!'"

Another day the great commander-in-chief rode
by as Hamilton was constructing some earth works
at Fort Washington.   He stopped his horse and
watched the little engineer.   And when he saw

that it was the captain who had drilled the artillery company so well, he invited him to his tent.

They had a long and delightful talk together. Young Hamilton sat on a camp stool answering questions ; he was so modest and intelligent that he quite won the heart of Washington ; and from that very day a friendship began between George Washington and Alexander Hamilton such as few men ever know. It was a friendship that lasted till death.

Some time you will read all about the war between the British and the Americans. I can only mention a few of the battles in this little book.

The king's troops seized New York. Then they followed Washington's army up the Hudson, and there were several engagements. Hamilton was always in the thickest of the fight. At Fort Washington he held the enemy back with his guns for a time; and when they had captured the fort, he hurried into the presence of Washington and proposed to re-capture it with his company. As he stood there with his cocked hat in his hand, he looked very eager and impatient to hurry to the task. But the prudent general thought the risk was too great, and ordered a retreat.

Hamilton soon won the name of the "Little Lion" by his boldness. He gloried in fighting for liberty. It is said that as he marched along beside his cannon, with his hand resting on the barrel, he patted and stroked it as if it were a favorite horse.

Washington kept on retreating toward Philadelphia. His army was poorly clothed and half fed and only numbered about three thousand men. Following after it came the great British army, under Cornwallis. There were over eight thousand soldiers in scarlet and gold, with banners flying and music playing; they were certain of victory.

When Washington reached the Raritan River, Cornwallis was close behind; but Hamilton planted his cannon on a high ledge of rocks above the ford of the river, and kept back the red coats until the rear of the ragged Americans was safe.

The "Little Lion" was soon rewarded for his pluck; he was appointed aide-de-camp and private secretary to General Washington, and he was given the rank of lieutenant-colonel; that was a proud day for Alexander Hamilton.

VI.—Washington's Aide-de-camp.

When General Washington received Colonel Hamilton into service as his private secretary, he said: "It will be a hard place to fill; I take no amusement for myself, and am busy from morning till night; I shall expect my secretary to be always at my side, ready to do his duty."

"I shall be prepared, your Excellency, to do your slightest bidding," answered Hamilton; and he kept his word. He wrote letters to the governors of the colonies for recruits, and to the commissaries for food and clothing; he wrote so much and so wisely that it was said, "The pen of the army is held by Hamilton."

He rode to Congress with secret despatches; he took orders to the different American generals, and, after a battle, he went to the camp of the British to treat for the exchange of prisoners.

General Washington trusted him completely and fondly called him "my boy."

Hamilton was then twenty years old, and Washington was forty-five.

At the battle of Brandywine, the young aide-de-camp rode to the front in the greatest danger to watch the enemy ; he carried despatches from one general to another. When his horse was shot under him, he hurried forward on foot.

After the terrible battle was over, the defeated American army retreated to Westchester. Hamilton rode all night by the side of the silent commander-in-chief. It was a sad night; the stars seemed to be mocking as they twinkled in the sky.

It was certain that, after their victory at Brandywine, the British would occupy Philadelphia ; and so, before they might reach there, Hamilton was sent to the city to ask for blankets, clothing, and food for the American army. He wrote such a charming letter to the ladies of the "Quaker City" that they gladly gave what they could, and his wagons were loaded and driven away before the drum beats of the British were heard.

Then Washington's army went into winter quarters at Valley Forge.

Now, the people who stayed at home were getting very tired of the war. Their fields were overrun by both armies, and their towns were burned by the enemy.

The British general issued a proclamation offering pardon to all who would swear allegiance to the king. He said that the property of faithful subjects would be spared, but the homes of the "rebels" should be burned to the ground.

Very many whigs were frightened into being tories; and when they had once become tories, they wanted the king's troops to conquer. They knew very well that if the Americans won, they themselves would be forever disgraced. And so they plotted to defeat them.

Then some of the American generals became jealous of Washington. They tried to remove him from command. But Hamilton was always watchful, and found out their schemes in time to prevent any harm.

Hamilton was loved by the soldiers in camp. Those who lay wounded waited for his coming,

because he knew so well how to bandage their
shattered limbs, and could write such beautiful
letters to their loved ones at home.

Hamilton was popular with the officers, too.
He was so genial and frank that they did not
envy him his high favor with the commander-in-
chief.

Among the officers was the Marquis de Lafayette. He was a Frenchman of noble birth, who had
given up all the pleasures of the French court at
Paris to help the Americans fight for liberty.
But he did not understand the English language
very well. Now, Hamilton had never forgotten the French language he had learned
from his mother. And so Lafayette and Hamilton became great friends, and talked much
together as they sat before the camp fire at
Valley Forge.

Another of Hamilton's friends was the Baron
von Steuben, a German, who also talked French.
The sturdy old general drilled the awkward
squads of continental soldiers, and he saw with
delight how eager young Hamilton was to master
the rules of war.

VII.—HAMILTON THE PATRIOT, AND ARNOLD THE TRAITOR.

The war of the Revolution went on, year after year. Sometimes the Americans and sometimes the British were victorious.

After a time, the French king, Louis XVI., sent over a fleet to help the Americans.

Then the most of the British army marched to the South. They hoped that the tories and the negroes would rally to their aid.

But the British General Clinton tarried in New York. He had great plans about enlisting the French and Indians of Canada to conquer the North. "If only I might get possession of West Point!" he said.

Now, West Point was the strongest fort in the colonies. Its frowning walls guarded the Hudson River. The British general knew very well that he could not bring the armies from Canada unless he controlled the Hudson River.

It is sad to relate that General Clinton found a traitor in the American army who was willing to betray West Point for gold!

Benedict Arnold was a brilliant young soldier

from Connecticut. He was so brave that he was promoted to the rank of major-general, and, after the British had retreated from Philadelphia, he was placed in command of the city.

When Arnold married the beautiful daughter of a rich tory, he wanted to make her happy; but, as we shall see, he really made her the most miserable lady in the world.

He began to live like a prince, in the great mansion that William Penn had built. He gave balls and fine dinners, and rode in a coach-and-four. But he needed more money to live so well.

" I will take money belonging to the army," he said, " and then I will pay it back as soon as I can. No one shall ever know anything about it." So he spent the money of the army. It was easy for such a high officer to get all the money he wanted.

At last Arnold spent more than he could ever pay back. His dishonesty was discovered. He was tried in court and found guilty, but his bravery had been so great that his punishment was made as light as possible.

Arnold seemed soon to forget his disgrace. He still gave large dinners at the elegant home in Philadelphia. Perhaps his rich father-in-law gave him money for this.

After a time he begged to be appointed commander of West Point, and was placed in charge of the great fort that guarded the Hudson River. Alas! he had already plotted to betray it to the British!

At midnight, in a lonely spot, he met Major André, the agent of General Clinton. Only the stars looked down upon him as he told how the fort might be seized if the British would pay him gold.

Soon after this, while Arnold was completing his plot, General Washington came to West Point with General Lafayette and Colonel Hamilton. He sent word to Arnold that he would make him a visit. Washington was delayed by some officers, and Hamilton rode with his apology to Mrs. Arnold.

Breakfast was served. Hamilton was charmed with the wit and grace of Mrs. Arnold, but he saw that Arnold was gloomy and silent. Indeed, the traitor was very wretched. He feared Washington's unexpected visit to the fort might spoil all his plans.

While he sat toying with his fork and trying in vain to be gay, a swift messenger arrived. He whispered in the traitor's ear that Major André had been arrested and a map of West Point found in his boot.

The unhappy man excused himself from the table. He called his wife to another room. He explained to her that his fortunes were ruined, and, mounting his horse, he fled.

Hamilton lifted the fainting wife from the floor, called a servant to care for her, and then hastened to General Washington. Washington sent him with all speed to cut off the traitor's retreat; but Arnold was already safe in a British ship.

Major André was hanged as a spy. Arnold, the traitor, lived to put the torch and the sword to many towns of his native land.

"Whom shall we trust now?" asked Washington sadly, as he thought of Benedict Arnold. But we know that Washington trusted Alexander Hamilton, and we shall see that his trust was never betrayed.

VIII.—THE LAWYER.

Colonel Hamilton met and loved Elizabeth Schuyler, the daughter of General Schuyler, one of the richest men in New York. Their marriage increased the young officer's reputation and added much to his social position.

Very soon after marriage, Hamilton resigned his place as aide-de-camp to General Washington, on account of a misunderstanding. It happened in the following way : One day, Washington passed Hamilton on the stairs and said, " I would like to speak with you, Colonel."

" I will wait upon your Excellency immediately," replied Hamilton, and went below to deliver some important letters to the postman.

As he returned, General Lafayette stopped to speak with him. Hamilton was very impatient ; he talked rapidly, and finally left the Frenchman abruptly. He searched for Washington in his room ; he was not there.

At last he found him at the head of the stairs. The great commander-in-chief looked stately and severe.

" Colonel Hamilton," he said, " you have kept

me waiting these ten minutes! I must tell you, sir, that you treat me with disrespect."

The face of the young aide-de-camp flushed as he heard the reproving words.

"I am not conscious of it, sir," he replied; "but since you have thought it necessary to tell me so, we part."

"Very well, sir, if it be your choice," said Washington.

The two friends parted in anger. In less than an hour General Washington sent word to Hamilton that he hoped the misunderstanding might be forgotten. Their friendship was continued.

No doubt both men were deeply grieved over their hasty words. But Hamilton had already written out his resignation; he felt he might find a greater field for work. He was soon placed in command of a regiment, and went to the South to join General Lafayette against the British.

The war raged furiously all through the South. At last General Washington himself came from the North with his army. The British at York-town were surrounded by land and by sea.

A siege was begun; and then Colonel Hamilton

distinguished himself by a very daring deed. Behind a high redoubt lay the guns of the British. Washington said the guns must be taken. Hamilton was named as the leader in an assault; he placed his foot on the shoulder of a sentinel, and was the first to mount the wall; he stood for a moment in full sight of the enemy's guns, calling aloud to his men.

Then he sprang into the ditch below, followed by his devoted soldiers with bayonets fixed. He pressed on past the British sentinels, and, in nine minutes' time, the American flag was floating over the parapet. You may be sure that Washington was proud of his young friend.

Very soon after this, the British surrendered to the American troops, and the long seven years' war was over.

The British army sailed away; Washington bade farewell to his officers, and retired to his home at Mount Vernon.

Hamilton went to Albany to live. He began to study law; in a few months he was able to pass his examinations, and was admitted to the bar.

Now, before the war most of the lawyers were

tories; and after the war they were not allowed
to practice in the courts. Thus it came about that
Hamilton found a large field for his new profession. He soon had more cases than he could
attend to.

There was only one lawyer in the state of New
York who seemed to be his equal; this was Aaron
Burr, a grandson of Jonathan Edwards, the great
preacher of New England.

Burr was a year older than Hamilton; he was
handsome and brave, and elegant in his manners.

He had been in the war, and was once a member of Washington's staff.

Washington disliked Burr, and did not keep
him long in his service.

Almost everybody admired him, but very few
trusted him, because he was dishonorable in his
dealings with men.

It often happened that Burr and Hamilton were
on different sides in a question of law. Sometimes
one and sometimes the other won the case at
court.

People began to say that the two young lawyers would soon be rivals in politics.

IX.—The Statesman.

Not long after Hamilton began the practice of law, he was elected a member from New York to the Continental Congress. Here he did what he could.

But the old Continental Congress had served its purpose; it had done very well for war; it would not do for peace. There was no President; there was no Supreme Court. Even the Congress itself was without any real authority. The little states were jealous of the big states, and the delegates were going home, one by one. Everybody said there would soon be no Congress at all.

Now, just at this very time there was more need of a strong government than ever before.

The paper dollars which Congress had issued were refused in payment of debts. People said the dollars were "not worth a continental," which meant they were not worth anything at all.

Indeed, everything continental seemed worthless. The Continental Congress had borrowed money from France, Holland, and Spain, and these countries clamored in vain for their pay.

The continental flag could not protect American commerce; the pirates in the Mediterranean Sea plundered the American ships, and British sailors boarded them; and the Spaniards at New Orleans refused to allow the Mississippi River to be navigated by Americans.

The continental army was disbanded; and when Congress taxed the states to raise some money, there were riots everywhere.

The kings of Europe began to rejoice at the distress of the Americans. "See," they said to their subjects, "see what a ridiculous spectacle a republic makes of itself! A kingdom is a firm and stable government; a republic is the rule of a mob."

England said that if the republic were only let alone it would fall to pieces of its own weight, and soon one state after another would be knocking at the door of Parliament to ask protection against her neighbors. And so King George kept his troops in the forts along the St. Lawrence. He hoped to win his colonies back again.

Hamilton urged Congress to call a convention of delegates from all the states to agree upon a better plan of government.

Now, there was so much quarreling in Congress that Hamilton could get little attention, and he soon resigned his office to practice law. But he watched and waited for the time when he might again propose a convention.

At last he was sent as a delegate to a commercial meeting at Annapolis. Here he urged his plan for a more perfect union. James Madison, of Virginia, helped him, and it was decided to ask Congress to call a convention to revise the articles of confederation.

Congress agreed to do this; and so, in May, 1787, a convention met at Philadelphia to form a permanent union between the states.

It was a noted body of men. There was George Washington, the hero of the Revolution; Robert Morris, the great merchant prince, who had almost spent his fortune that the armies might be fed; Benjamin Franklin, who had just returned from the court of the French king; Edmund Randolph, who had refused to sail away in a tory ship with his father; and James Madison, who would one day be President.

There were governors, lawyers, and merchants

among these delegates at Philadelphia, but among them all none was more ready for work than Alexander Hamilton.

He had a plan of government already formed in his own mind, and wished to persuade the rest to adopt it.

George Washington was elected president of the convention, and then the debates began.

Now, all agreed that there should be a union of the states, but there were many different opinions about what this union should be.

Some wanted a government with each state independent, except in time of war. Others wanted a government with all the states firmly united. A few, who had been made timid by the riots, declared that only a king could keep peace.

The convention lasted four months, and the debates were loud and long. Many times the meeting was almost broken up, and the talk grew so bitter that Franklin moved prayer be said every morning.

Hamilton was kept very busy. Once he spoke five hours without stopping. He proposed a strong government, with a President, a Congress, and a

Supreme Court, much as we have it now. Some day, in a larger book, you will read all about it.

In the end, the *Constitution of the United States* was written and signed. Washington's name was first on the list. The great general held his pen in his hand as he said: "Should the states reject this excellent Constitution, the probability is that an opportunity will never again offer to cancel another in peace. The next will be drawn in blood." Franklin said: "I consent, sir, to this Constitution because I expect no better, and because I am not sure it is not the best."

No one has told what Hamilton said, but we can see his name standing out, firm and clear, on the yellow parchment which lies under glass in the capitol at Washington.

After the Constitution was properly signed by the delegates, it was submitted to the old Continental Congress. The Congress agreed to let the states say whether they wished to adopt the new government.

If nine states adopted it, a union would be formed. All the states called conventions to consider the question.

X.—The Federalist.

Of course, the people were sure to disagree about the new Constitution. Governors in the states did not like to have a President who would be greater than they. Militias in the states did not want to be at the beck and call of a President who would be their commander-in-chief. Judges in the states did not care to have their decisions appealed to a supreme court. Merchants did not choose to allow a Congress to put taxes on the goods they imported from Europe.

And so there was a great deal of talking.

Those who favored the Constitution were called federalists, and those who opposed it were called anti-federalists.

Some great patriots were anti-federalists. Patrick Henry of Virginia was an anti-federalist, because he feared the President and Congress might take liberty from the people.

Samuel Adams, of Massachusetts, was an anti-federalist, because he feared one government could not hold so many states together.

Now, this old patriot had much influence.

People said Massachusetts would vote against the Constitution if Samuel Adams did.

But some workingmen met in the Green Dragon Tavern in Boston. It was their opinion that if the Constitution was not ratified their trades would be ruined. A committee bore their resolutions to Samuel Adams; and Paul Revere, who had aroused the sleeping towns for the battle of Lexington, handed him the paper.

"How many mechanics were at the Green Dragon?" asked Adams.

"More, sir, than the Green Dragon could hold," answered Paul Revere.

"And where were the rest, Mr. Revere?"

"In the streets, sir."

"And how many were in the streets?"

"More, sir, than there are stars in the sky."

And because Samuel Adams had faith in the judgment of the industrious workingmen, he resolved from that moment to be a federalist.

Nothing that anybody could say changed the mind of Governor George Clinton, of New York. He opposed the Constitution with all his might.

Alexander Hamilton urged the adoption of the Constitution. He wrote, with John Jay, of New York, and James Madison, of Virginia, a series of essays called the Federalist. The Federalist explained the new plan of government.

It had great influence all over the country. But there were so many anti-federalists in New York that people said the state would never adopt the Constitution.

There was talking from morning till night in the taverns and on the corners of the streets.

Hamilton hardly slept or ate, he was so busy trying to persuade the people to agree to the Constitution. At last news came that eight states had ratified it.

When the New York convention met to vote, there was the greatest excitement. Only one more state was needed to make the Constitution a law. Would New Hampshire vote for it? Would Virginia vote for it? Hamilton sent off couriers for reports from these two states. The days seemed very long.

At last a courier came riding at full speed. "New Hampshire has ratified!" he shouted.

" Hurrah!" answered the friends of the Constitution, and they hurried to tell that the new government was established.

Would New York join the union, or remain independent? Everybody was asking the question. Now, New York, at that time, was not so great in either wealth or population as Virginia, Massachusetts, or Pennsylvania. But the state was very important, for all that. There it lay, dividing New England from the middle and southern states. You can see very well that, if New York had stayed out of the union, she might have been a troublesome neighbor to the United States of America.

Hamilton argued in the convention while waiting for reports from Virginia. "Let others try the experiment first," said Governor Clinton and his friends. Everybody said that, if Virginia refused to ratify, New York would be sure to follow her example.

It took a long time for news to come from far away Virginia. But at last a horseman brought tidings that Virginia, the "mother of the colonies," had adopted the Constitution.

"Hurrah! hurrah!" shouted the friends of the Constitution. "What will our convention do now?" they asked.

The excitement of the crowds outside the courthouse waxed greater than ever. "Hamilton is speaking!" went from mouth to mouth. "Hamilton is speaking yet! He has changed more votes!"

And when the news was carried to the people that their convention had ratified the Constitution, a shout went up all over the state. There was a holiday to celebrate the event. Cannons boomed, bells rang, and thousands marched in line in the streets of New York city.

The portrait of Hamilton with the Constitution in his hand was carried in the parade; a small frigate, called the "Ship of State," bore the name Hamilton in large letters, and on the national flag were pictured the faces of Washington and Hamilton. The celebration closed with a public dinner, where toasts were offered in honor of Hamilton.

It was a proud day for the young federalist.

XI.—The First Secretary of the Treasury.

The people of the United States had now much to do. There were the Congressmen to be elected in all the states, and there were electors to be chosen to name a President.

George Washington, the hero of the Revolution, was elected President.

New York was made the capital; and when Washington stood on the balcony of the city hall to take the oath of office, Hamilton stood by his side, among other distinguished men.

When Chancellor Livingston exclaimed, " Long live George Washington, President of the United States!" cocked hats were tossed in the air, handkerchiefs fluttered, and above all waved the new flag of the Union, while thousands of voices shouted that the government had begun.

Soon the President asked Robert Morris: "What is to be done about this immense war debt of the United States?"

The great financier replied: " There is but one man in the United States who can tell you, and that man is Alexander Hamilton."

And so, when Washington appointed his

Cabinet, he made Hamilton Secretary of the Treasury.

As a member of the Cabinet, Hamilton had many social duties. He assisted at the President's levees and at the Friday evening receptions of "Lady Washington." The beauty and wit of the nation were there. The envoys from Europe stood about in brilliant uniforms; and the officers of the army and of the navy were there, with their swords and medals voted by Congress. But no man in all the throng was more observed than Alexander Hamilton.

He generally wore a blue coat, a white silk waist-coat, black trousers to the knee, and long, white silk stockings. His powdered hair was combed back and tied in a cue. Although below middle size, he was erect and dignified. His brow was lofty, his face was fair, his voice was musical, and his manner was frank and cordial.

But social duties were the least of Hamilton's duties. He was to restore the public credit at home and abroad and this must be done by raising money to pay the national debt.

Yet he knew very well that, if the people

were taxed too much, they would rebel against the government.

At last he persuaded Congress to put a high tariff on imported wares, and a tax on whisky and a few other home products. Then he had to oversee the collecting of the public money, and to pay it out again on the national debt.

He proposed a National Bank, and, after much debate, the Bank of the United States was established at Philadelphia. Then he recommended a mint. There were few American coins. English, French, and Spanish coins were about all the money we had. Congress ordered a mint to melt gold, silver, and copper, and stamp it.

People began to feel very proud of their country when they read "The United States of America" on the shining pieces of money.

The nations of Europe soon treated the American flag with more respect. They said the Republic seemed like a young giant. But they said, too, that young giants stumbled more easily than anybody else. They would wait a while before they believed that the new government would be a permanent one.

Hamilton continued to labor in all the departments of his office. He suggested laws for navigation and the coasting trade. He established bureaus for the sale of the lands in the West. He founded the United States Post-office. He made a report on American manufactures, and urged a high tax on foreign manufactures to encourage the home products.

And while he was toiling day and night, enemies attacked his character. They said he had used public money to bribe men for votes. A committee investigated the treasury books, but found that every dollar was in its place.

Hamilton was then more popular than ever; and when Washington was elected President for a second term, Hamilton was again chosen Secretary of the Treasury.

In 1795 he resigned his office, and resumed the practice of law in New York city. He was only thirty-eight years old, yet he had served his country for nearly twenty years, and won the name of the " founder of the public credit."

Many years after, Daniel Webster said: " Hamilton smote the rock of the national resources, and

abundant streams of revenue gushed forth. He touched the dead corpse of public credit, and it sprang upon its feet." Is not that high praise from a great orator to a great statesman?

XII.—INSPECTOR-GENERAL OF THE ARMY.

Hamilton was urged by his party to accept the nomination for governor of New York. He refused the honor. He preferred to practice law. He soon bought a small estate on the north end of Manhattan Island, and built a hospitable house, which he called the *Grange*, after the mansion of his grandfather in Scotland.

Here he was the center of a large circle of admiring friends. On another part of Manhattan lived Aaron Burr, his rival in politics and at the bar. Whatever Alexander Hamilton wished was sure to be opposed by Aaron Burr.

But talent and industry kept Hamilton far in the front. By his practice in the courts, he grew more famous than ever. The rich and the poor brought their troubles to the great lawyer. It is said that Washington still sought his advice in national affairs ; and then, as the President completed his second term of office, Hamilton helped him write the Farewell Address.

If you hear this famous Farewell Address read on Washington's birthday, perhaps you will think of Alexander Hamilton.

Now, when John Adams, of Massachusetts, became President, trouble was already brewing between the United States and France.

You remember how Louis XVI. sent a fleet to America to aid in the war against the British. It so happened that, very soon after, the king had a war with his own people. He was driven from his throne, and France became a republic.

"If one throne falls," said the other kings of Europe, "all thrones may fall ; we must not let the French establish a republic as the Americans have done"; and so the kings united to fight France. Then the Directory, which was the name of five men who ruled the new French republic, called across the sea to the Americans : "We helped you," they said, "when you fought for liberty; come and help us."

This was a stirring appeal. Republican clubs

were formed all over the United States ; they sang French songs and dressed after the French fashion. But while Washington was President, he had hesitated to take up arms against England ; he said the only two English-speaking nations on the globe should be friends.

It seemed unwise to take part in the quarrels of Europe. Besides, it was King Louis who sent help to America, and the French mobs had cut off the head of King Louis. Washington declared the United States would take no part in the wars of France.

When John Adams became President, he, too, said we should remain friends to all the nations of Europe. Then the French became very disagreeable ; they began to shoot at the flags on our ships. President Adams sent agents to Paris to try to arrange the difficulties ; but the French Directory insulted the agents, and ordered them out of the city. Of course, *all* the Americans were angry then. The Republican clubs took off their French badges, and quit singing French songs.

The President and Congress prepared for war. Washington was appointed lieutenant-general of the army, with Hamilton his first major-general. Ships were built ; armies were collected and drilled. There was hurrying everywhere. Meantime, Napoleon had become the ruler in France; and when he saw that the Americans were so eager to defend their honor, he treated them with more respect. After a time, peace was made between France and the United States.

Before peace had been concluded, the death of Washington caused mourning throughout the land. Hamilton became commander of the American armies, but he went about his duties with a very sad heart.

XIII.—ALEXANDER HAMILTON AND AARON BURR.

When all danger of war was over, Hamilton began again to practice law.

He withdrew more and more from public life. It is said that in the trial of his cases the great lawyer was almost always successful.

Sometimes he spoke many hours, but no one wished to leave the court-room until he had finished his speech.

Now, all this time Aaron Burr had been rising in power. He was crafty and revengeful; he did what he could to blacken the character of Hamilton. When the term of John Adams drew to a close, Aaron Burr became a candidate for President against Thomas Jefferson, of Virginia.

Hamilton used his great influence against the election of Burr. He thought him a man without honor, and therefore unfit for the high office to which he aspired.

When Jefferson was elected, Burr was very angry; he said that Hamilton had caused his defeat.

Then, when Burr wished to be governor of New York, he was defeated again. He was more angry than ever; he laid all the blame of failure on Hamilton; he brooded over his evil thoughts.

How might he get rid of this powerful man who stood in his way? He decided to kill him; but he said he would not, like a common murderer, kill him in the night; he would challenge him to fight a duel.

It is said that Burr trained his hand at shooting targets until he never missed his mark. When he was sure that he would not fail he sent a challenge to Hamilton.

In those days a duel was a common way to settle disputes. Hamilton had lost a dear son in a duel. He thought the custom of dueling was wrong; yet he knew very well that, if he did not accept the challenge, he would be called a coward.

"If war should ever break out again," he said, "who would trust a man in command, if he had ever been called a coward?"

And so he accepted Burr's challenge, but he asked that the duel be put off until he had finished his cases in that term of court. He did not wish others to suffer loss if he died.

The days went by; the great lawyer pleaded his cases, and attended to all his duties as usual.

Once, at a public dinner, when urged to sing his favorite song, he arose to his feet and sang the patriotic verses, one by one.

Just across the table sat Aaron Burr. His eyes were fixed on the glowing face of the singer. He whispered to himself : " It is the last time that the people of this nation shall listen to the voice of Alexander Hamilton."

XIV.—THE DUEL.

At dawn, on the eleventh day of July, 1804, the duel took place. The two men, with their seconds, met on the Jersey shore at Weehawken, opposite New York. Hamilton had said he would not fire the first round; he did not wish to kill his enemy. They measured paces. At the given word, Burr fired. Hamilton fell. Burr hastened away in a boat. He was soon condemned as a murderer, and fled for his life.

Hamilton was carried to his barge. He was placed on a cot, and borne to the house of a friend. A long line of citizens followed the almost lifeless body. They wept and wrung their hands. All felt that he must die. His wife and children were summoned; and, in a few hours, Alexander Hamilton breathed his last.

On the day of his funeral the business houses in New York City were closed. The flags on the ships in the harbor were hung at half-mast, and the bells of the churches were muffled and tolled.

A vast procession followed the hero to his grave. His war horse, with empty saddle, draped in black, walked behind the casket. Then came regiments of soldiers. Then the president and the students of Columbia College marched together, because the "orphan boy of Nevis" had been an honored student of Columbia College, when it was King's College. Behind the students marched the many societies, who wished to do honor to the dead; and all over the country there was mourning for the great financier, the soldier, the lawyer, and the statesman, Alexander Hamilton.

Ministers in their pulpits deplored his loss. One said: "Alexander Hamilton was a man on whom nature seemed to impress the stamp of greatness.

"He was the *hero* whose first appearance in the field conciliated the esteem of Washington; the *statesman* whose genius impressed itself upon the constitution of his country; the *patriot* whose integrity baffled the closest scrutiny, and the *counsellor* who was at once the pride of the bar and the admiration of the court.

"The name of Hamilton raises in the mind the idea of whatever is great, whatever is splendid, whatever is illustrious in human nature.

"Wherever Alexander Hamilton was, the friendless had a friend, the fatherless a father, and the poor man an advocate."

The newspapers were banded in black. Each paid loving tribute to the dead. Even those that had often opposed him hastened now to praise him.

"Americans!" said the Charleston *Courier*, "in Alexander Hamilton, you have lost your champion, your counsellor, and your guide.

"Who is there in the ancient or the modern world that has surpassed him? If we look to his life, we shall find more to praise and less to censure than in almost any other.

"The head that guided your guides—that clearest head that ever conceived, and that sweetest tongue that ever uttered, the dictates of wisdom—lies mouldering to clay; yet the deeds this great man wrought will live forever."

"The name of Hamilton will not die," said one newspaper, "until that dark day shall come when the name of Washington will also be remembered no more."

"No country ever deplored a greater man," said another.

" Behold!" said another, "a Washington and a Hamilton meet again in gladness and triumph."

The dust of the illustrious statesman lies in Trinity Churchyard, at the head of busy Wall Street. On a bluff of Manhattan stands the "Grange," once his country home, removed a short distance from where it then stood. But the thirteen trees still flourish where he planted them in remembrance of the thirteen states he had helped to unite into one great nation.

They tower high above the trees around them. It was thus, too, that the fame of Alexander Hamilton arose above that of other men.

Like Cain, who slew his brother, Aaron Burr, who slew America's greatest statesman, became a wanderer on the earth. The name of Hamilton sounded in his ears wherever he went.

"Ah, the slayer of *Hamilton!*" exclaimed an English lord, and cooly turned his back.

"I always have a miniature of *Hamilton* hanging over my mantle piece," replied a French statesman whose favor he sought.

" By the death of *Hamilton* you have forfeited

the right of citizenship," said a consul as he refused him passports.

Wearied with his treatment in Europe, Burr returned to New York city.

His old friends shunned him and strangers who heard his name refused to clasp his hand.

At last, when very old and very poor, he died; and the event served only to renew the universal praise of Alexander Hamilton.

THE STORY OF

ANDREW JACKSON

ANDREW JACKSON.

THE STORY OF ANDREW JACKSON.

I.—BIRTH.

Perhaps you have already heard something about General Andrew Jackson, and you may have seen the old soldier's portrait, or one of his statues which stand in parks and other public places.

Andrew Jackson was such a wonderful man, and did so much for our country, that I am sure you will be glad to read all that you can about him.

His father, whose name was also Andrew Jackson, was a poor farmer in Carrickfergus, on the north coast of Ireland.

He rented a few acres of land from a rich lord, who threatened, every time he could not pay his rent, to turn him out of his cabin. His wife was a sad-eyed little woman, who wove linen all day long; but, with their hardest work, they could barely get food enough for themselves and their children.

One day Jackson received a letter from a friend who had gone to America to live. The friend wrote that he could have his passage paid across the ocean, if he would only come to North Carolina, and build a home in the pine forest.

It was a long time before the poor farmer gave any heed to the letter.

He loved the peat bogs where he had always lived, and where his parents and grand-parents had lived before him, and he could not make up his mind to leave the kind neighbors who toiled and suffered like himself.

Then, perhaps, there was a failure of crops, or, perhaps, the rich landlord said something cruel about his rent—just why it was I do not know; but, in the end, he concluded to go to America.

And so Andrew Jackson, his wife and two boys, Hugh and Robert, took sail in an emigrant ship.

They landed at Charleston, in South Carolina, and went to the Waxhaw settlement in North Carolina, where their friend from old Ireland was living.

Now, this was in the year 1765, the very time when the Stamp Act was causing so much excitement in America. In all the towns along the coast the people were talking about the tyranny of King George of England.

But Andrew Jackson did not hear very much about the king or the Stamp Act. He was busy felling trees and planting corn. He was proud to call the little farm his own, and thought that America was the most wonderful country in the world.

His wife picked the wild flax, and spun and wove it into cloth; and the bloom came back to her cheeks, and she sang all day long as she worked at the wheel.

But sorrow soon came to her even in this land of plenty and song. In two years Andrew Jackson died.

A few days after, on the 15th of March, 1767, another son was born.

He was a wee, frail baby, and his wails mingled with the sound of mourning for the husband, who slept on the hillside.

"I will call him Andrew," said the weeping mother. "Perhaps he will grow handsome and strong, like his father!"

II.—BOYHOOD.

When Andrew was three weeks old, his mother
moved across the border, from North Carolina
into South Carolina, where her brother lived.

"He'll never stand the journey," said the good
women of the neighborhood, as he was bundled
up with shawls, and put away in a basket.

But the journey was made, although the rough
winds blew, and Andy was soon unloaded at his
uncle's door.

"He'll not live to feel his first tooth!" croaked
the good women of this new neighborhood.

But Andrew kept growing in spite of all they
said. He clinched his little fists at colic, measles,
and whooping cough. He talked very early, and
walked instead of crawled, and set the whole
house in a roar if any one chanced to take liberties
with his toys.

"If you ask me for things, you may have them,"
he said, "but you shall not touch them without my
leave."

"Touchy!" sniffed his brothers, but they did not
often cross him because he was so much younger
than themselves.

When Andy was old enough, he went to school with his brothers. Little did the master think, as he peered over his spectacles, that he was looking at a future President of the United States.

Andy seemed timid and modest. He was tall and thin; his head was long and narrow; his face was pale, and about it hung thin hair as white as flax. But what eyes the child had! They were a clear blue, that flashed like steel in the sun.

" The lad looks too meek for this earth," said the kind hearted teacher to himself. He patted Andy's flaxen head and gave him a seat on the lowest bench.

Andy showed his mettle the very first time that a lubberly fellow teased him. He could not strike back with his puny fists, but, while the master was busy, he shaped a big boy out of paper. Then, with a grim gesture of warning, he fastened a paper string about the paper boy's neck, and flung him dangling from the bench. It was soon noised about the school that Andy Jackson was too savage to be teased.

He showed no end of pluck. " We can throw

him three times out of four," said his mates, " but he'll never *stay* thrown."

" Easy, lad, easy," said the master, one day, as he caught the little spitfire in the act of rushing upon a playmate. " Thou'llt have others to fight besides thy school-fellows, if I read the signs aright."

At this very time strange news was creeping up the valley of the Waxhaw. British soldiers were trying to make the Americans obey unjust laws and people were saying there would soon be war.

Then tidings of the battle of Lexington came.

Andy was not sure where Lexington was, but he knew that Americans lived there, and that the British king had sent over troops to fight them.

That was quite enough to know. He had heard from his mother how the cruel lords of Ireland oppressed the poor, and he was furious because the king's laws were making Americans suffer like the Irish.

He stamped round and round the little log

cabin where he lived; he fastened the steel of a
scythe to a pole, and mowed down the tall weeds
in a rage.

"Out with the tyrants!" he cried. "Oh, if I were
a man now, how I would sweep down the British
with my grass blade!"

Word came that South Carolina had raised
troops to resist the British soldiers. Then one
courier brought news that the king's governor had
fled to his ships in the harbor; and then another
courier rode in haste to tell how the fleet at
Charleston had been driven out to sea.

It was hard work to study in those days;
even the master was unlike himself. He wandered about the room as if he could not keep
quiet.

And one hot July morning when Andy reached
the school, he found the door shut. What did it
mean? The road was full of wagons and horsemen. They were all going one way.

Andy followed the crowd and reached the court
house. He heard men talk of a "Declaration of
Independence."

Now, he was only nine years old, and did not

understand just what a Declaration of Independence was; but when men threw up their hats and made the woods ring with their shouts he was quite sure it was a good thing, and he, too, threw up his cap of coon-skin and shouted with all his might.

After this I am sure that the bench at school saw very little of Andy Jackson.

He hung about the blacksmith shop, which stood in a clearing near his house, to watch the men of Carolina fashion old saws into swords and melt pewter mugs into bullets.

And as they worked they told how General Washington had been defeated at Brandywine, and how a British general had surrendered at Saratoga.

Men came very often up the Waxhaw with news from the battlefields.

When, at last, Andy heard of the surrender of Charleston to the British, he could not rest at home.

He mounted his horse and rode off with his brothers to join a party of scouts in pursuit of the British redcoats.

III.—The Young Prisoner of War.

Andrew was now thirteen years old and as tall as a man. He was fearless and bold, and none more than he won renown as a scout.

About this time Tarleton, the British general, raided the settlements on Waxhaw Creek. He bribed and frightened many of Jackson's neighbors to join his army.

He pinned a red rag on their coats to show that they favored the British; but you may be sure that no red rag was pinned to the coat of Andrew Jackson.

He and his brothers escaped to the woods, and fought their foes as long as they could.

At last Robert and Andrew were captured. When a haughty officer ordered Andrew to black his boots, he stood proudly before the scowling redcoat and said: "Sir, I am a prisoner of war, and demand to be treated as such."

"Impudence!" shouted the officer. " Black the boots instantly."

The slim boy drew himself up; his eyes blazed like fire as he cried: "I am not a servant to any Briton that breathes!"

The officer struck at him with a sword. He parried the blow with his hand, but bore the scars to the end of his life.

Hugh died from neglect of wounds received in a battle. Andrew and Robert were taken to the town of Camden, which the British had captured.

They were kept, with nearly three hundred other Americans, in an open field surrounded by a high board fence.

Disease soon killed many, and starvation killed more.

Their only hope was that some American troops would come to rescue them from what seemed worse than death itself.

At last, they heard the sentinels say that General Greene was marching toward Camden.

There was great excitement in the little pen over this news. All day the prisoners wandered about the high fence, peering at every splinter to find an opening where they might see out.

At night, Andrew pried a knot from a board. He waited anxiously for the first peep of dawn.

When, at last, the friendly light came, he stood at the opening and spied an army on Hobkirk's

Hill. He knew the men were Americans by their blue and buff uniforms, and by their flag with its thirteen bars of red and white and its thirteen stars on a field of blue.

His heart beat fast as he saw this new American banner fluttering over the general's tent. He let others climb up to get a peep at it. One of the stars was for South Carolina. How the prisoners longed to leap over the fence and fight for that star!

But British guards stood outside the enclosure. The unhappy prisoners could only huddle in a bunch to hear Andrew tell what he saw outside.

While General Greene was waiting for cannon, his soldiers were busy with their morning chores. Some were stirring fires under great pots to boil their breakfasts; some were washing linen in the little stream that ran at the foot of the hill; some were polishing muskets, and some were playing games.

One tall officer came out of headquarters, and, mounting his horse, rode from tent to tent.

"That must be General Greene himself!" shouted Andrew in a hoarse whisper.

"Hurrah! give us a squint at him, Andy," said the waiting men.

"Yes, that is he, sure enough," said one. "You can tell him by his straps."

"Greene was with Washington at Brandywine," said another.

"Aye," said another, "and he helped capture the Dutch at Trenton on a Christmas!"

They scrambled over each other to catch a glimpse of the hero. "Where's our Marion, the 'Swamp Fox'?"

"Can't see him, but if he's not there he's somewhere else!"

Suddenly, in the midst of the whispers, there sounded a clash of arms and a stamping of horses back of the prison fence.

"What's that? What's that?" now fairly shouted the startled men.

Andrew was at the knot-hole again; he saw the British General Rawdon leading his troopers out to surprise the camp. They rode very fast, with loud hurrahs, as if they had already won the battle.

The Americans made a rush for arms in the tents. Then they rallied, and swept down the hill at Rawdon's rear.

The prisoners fairly shouted now. What did it matter if the sentinels heard?

Many rushed pell-mell toward the door of the prison, expecting to be free in the wink of an eye.

But Andrew stood close to the knot-hole; he saw how horses ran riderless, how the bluecoats were mowed down by the redcoats, and how, at last, Greene and his men retreated beyond the other side of Hobkirk's Hill.

When the sound of the pursuing army died away, the prisoners fell back in despair. It seemed as if they would never escape from the prison pen.

Now, all this time Mrs. Jackson had been trying to find her boys. When she reached Camden, she so moved the hearts of the officers by her tears that they exchanged Andrew and Robert for some British prisoners. Her arms were soon around the poor lads.

Robert was so ill that he was placed on a horse; the mother rode another horse. Andrew was gaunt and pale; he was without jacket or shoes, and so weak that he could hardly stand, yet he walked behind the horses; and thus the three plodded over forty miles to their old home.

Then both boys fell ill with the smallpox. Robert died, but Andrew recovered.

When news came of disease among the American prisoners in the harbor of Charleston, Andrew's mother resolved to go as a nurse to the pest-laden ships. She arrived at Charleston, but soon after died of the fever; and so Andrew Jackson, at the age of fifteen, was left all alone in the world.

IV.—The Lawyer.

About the time Andrew's mother died, Cornwallis, the British general, surrendered his army to Washington at Yorktown, and soon all the red coats withdrew from the southern states.

The American families who had fled to the forests for safety returned to their homes on the coast. Among these were some young men whom Jackson knew.

After they had gone he was so lonesome that he sold his little homestead and followed them to Charleston. There he fell in with some wild fellows and wasted his money. He soon saw the folly of this and began to take life more seriously.

First he worked as an apprentice in a saddler's shop, but he much preferred riding in a saddle to making one. Then he taught school for a time, but could not endure to be penned in with dullards and drones; so he mounted his horse and rode to Salisbury, North Carolina, to study law.

The king's lawyers had fled the country during the war and there was a fine opening in the courts for young Americans.

Alexander Hamilton and Aaron Burr had just begun their practice before the bar in New York, and John Quincy Adams was preparing to return from Europe in order to enter Harvard College.

Others who would one day become noted lawyers were Henry Clay, a boy of seven, in the "slashes" of Virginia; Daniel Webster and Lewis Cass, of New Hampshire; John C. Calhoun, of South Carolina; Thomas H. Benton, of North Carolina; and Martin Van Buren, of New York. These last were toddling infants two years old; yet they were destined to be friends or foes to the Irish immigrant's son.

Jackson was seventeen years old when he began to study law. He was tall and slim; his face was long and thin, with a high, narrow forehead; his eyes were deep blue, and his glance was open and frank.

He made many friends in his new home. Indeed, all through life he found friends wherever he went, because he was honest, generous, and true.

Now, while Andrew Jackson, the raw country lad, was studying law in Salisbury, some men, whom you know very well, were busy trying to form a government.

There was no government of the United States at that time as there is now. Each state still governed itself.

The Continental Congress, which had kept the states together during the war, was falling to pieces.

"Something must be done to form a government," said the patriots who had struggled to save the country.

And George Washington, John Adams, Benjamin Franklin, and others wrote letters and made speeches about the need of a permanent union among the states.

Perhaps it was hearing some of these noble men talk that set Andrew Jackson to thinking more seriously than ever. He studied law in earnest, and succeeded so well that in 1788 he was appointed public prosecutor for the Western District of North Carolina.

V.—The District Attorney.

The Western District of North Carolina lay beyond the Blue Ridge Mountains. It was a vast wilderness where Indians still lived, but it was being slowly settled by the white men.

Whenever Jackson saw the rough hunters come into Salisbury to sell their packs of skins, he questioned them about the West; the more he heard of it, the more he thought he would like to go there.

And so when he was made public prosecutor for the land beyond the mountains, he gladly set out with a hundred other adventurers.

Pack horses carried their tents and cooking vessels, and all the men had rifles. They passed through Cumberland Gap and were soon in a vast forest. Danger lurked on every side. Scouts

went in advance all day, and sentinels stood guard
while their comrades slept.

One night, after the camp was silent, Jackson
was lying against a tree enjoying the cool breeze.
when he heard an owl hooting in the distance.
Soon another owl hooted.

"There are many owls in these woods," he
thought.

Then another owl, with a strange hoarseness in
its call, hooted quite near the camp. Jackson
started from his seat; he glided over to a friend,
and touched him gently.

"What's the matter?" growled the sleeper.

"Listen!" whispered Jackson. "Hear the owls!"

"You're not afraid of owls, Jackson?" said his
friend, with a laugh.

"But listen to that again! It's *too* natural. It's
Indians; I'm sure of it. They're giving signals
and gathering about us."

The two aroused some hunters, who declared
that Indians were near. Tents were quickly
packed, and the company moved silently on.

That very night some passing hunters, who
found the deserted camp-fire, lay down to sleep,

and before dawn all but one were killed by the Indians.

Jackson's party traveled through great forests, where the leaves were turning red and yellow, and at the end of October reached Nashville, on the Cumberland River.

The settlers read the letters they had brought in their saddle-bags, and questioned them eagerly about everything in the states.

When they heard that the majority of the colonies had adopted the Constitution of the United States, and that electors were to choose a president, they said George Washington, of Virginia, would be elected; and, surely enough, he was, in April, 1789.

Soon after the election, news was brought that the western district of North Carolina had been ceded to the United States, and called the South-west Territory, and that President Washington had appointed Andrew Jackson to be the district attorney.

Now the district attorney was a very important officer. Many who moved to the West had forgotten to pay their debts, and it was the attorney's duty to remind them of it; he had to punish for land stealing and horse stealing, and to settle drunken quarrels.

Court day was the greatest day of the year. Friends and foes met then, and almost as many quarrels were begun as were settled.

When the offenders were not satisfied with the decision of the court, they would often hurry from the house and fight out the dispute, with the judge and jury looking on.

Jackson went on horseback from one court-house to another. He was in constant danger from the Indians, but he was in almost as much danger from those whom he punished.

When bullets whizzed past him in the forest, he laughingly said: "A miss is as good as a mile!" And the more he was persecuted, the more he was determined to stay at Nashville.

VI.—THE CONGRESSMAN.

In 1791, Andrew Jackson married Rachel Robards. She was a bright-eyed beauty whose father had been one of the wealthiest men on the frontier. They lived very happily together.

In 1792, the territory just north of Jackson's district was admitted to the Union and called Kentucky.

Then people in the Southwest Territory began to talk about organizing a state government and joining the Union.

"If Kentucky can send its representatives to the Congress at Philadelphia, why can't we?" said Jackson and his friends.

There was much talking about the matter on court days and at log rollings and corn huskings.

At last, with a deep sense of the important steps they were to take, delegates oiled their hair with bear's grease, and donned their best buckskins.

With muskets in their hands and bowie-knives in their belts, they pushed through the wintry woods to Knoxville, a thriving little village on the Holston River.

Among those who went none had more influence than Andrew Jackson. In the court house at Knoxville, where the logs were piled high in the great fire-place, he helped to frame the constitution for a state.

"What shall we name our state?" asked these
lawmakers. "Let its name be Tennessee, after
the river—the 'River with the great Bend,'" said
Jackson. Then messengers took the constitution
to Philadelphia, to ask Congress to admit Tennessee into the Union.

Now at this time there were two political
parties. The Federalist party feared to give too
much power to the masses of the people, and the
Republican party feared the power of the learned
and rich.

Alexander Hamilton and the Federalists declared that the United States government was
not yet stable enough to allow a crowd of Western
ruffians to send delegates to Congress.

But Aaron Burr and the Republicans said that
they would risk the rough frontiersmen any time
sooner than the aristocrats of the cities.

The Republicans had their way, and Tennessee
was admitted to the Union as the sixteenth state.
Then who should be elected the first representa-
tive in Congress? "Andrew Jackson!" shouted
almost everybody in Tennessee.

And so the new congressman mounted his horse

and set out on the journey to Philadelphia, nearly eight hundred miles away.

When he reached the capital city, he seemed quite out of place. He was tall and lank; his hair hung over his face and was tied at the back in an eel-skin; his dress was peculiar, and there were many rumors afloat about his rude life in the West.

When he attempted to make a speech, he choked and hesitated ; but for all that, he helped pass a bill to repay the people of Tennessee for the expenses of an Indian war. This made him more popular at home than ever.

He was soon chosen a senator ; and among the very first to greet him in the Senate was Aaron Burr, who had helped pass the Indian Bill. The two men became great friends, and their friendship lasted as long as they lived.

Jackson did not like to live in Philadelphia, and soon resigned his position to go back home. He had already seen much while in office. He had seen President Washington enter the Chamber of Representatives to deliver his last address. He had seen John Adams inaugurated President, and he had met Thomas Jefferson and James Madison, who would some day be presidents.

But little did the rough frontiersman think that he himself would ever be President, and little did any one else think it, either !

VII.—Storekeeper, Judge, and Planter.

When Jackson returned to Tennessee, he brought with him a train of packhorses loaded with goods. He built a cabin in Clover Bottom, near Nashville, and filled it with farming imple- ments, salt, sugar, blankets, cotton and woolen goods, and many other things.

Then he exchanged these wares for skins, raw cotton, corn, wheat, and pork to send down the Mississippi to New Orleans, where he received good Spanish dollars in exchange.

People came many miles to trade at the store in Clover Bottom. Indians came, but they were such thieves that Jackson did not allow them to enter the store. He made them stand in a row at a win- dow, through which he handed out their supplies.

After a time, Andrew Jackson was appointed judge of the supreme court of Tennessee and major-general of the militia, and he built a fine house and lived in style.

Then he was unfortunate in business. He had to sell his fine house and most of his land to pay his debts, and he moved back to the little log cabin where he had first begun housekeeping.

"Rather go to bed supperless than to rise in debt," was Andrew Jackson's motto.

He held his good name higher than anything else. His reputation for honor was so great that men always trusted him. When a citizen of Tennessee wanted a loan from a banker in Boston, he showed the names of many prominent men in his state.

"Do you know Andrew Jackson?" asked the banker.

"Yes, but he is not worth a tenth as much as either of these men whose names I offer you."

"No matter," replied the shrewd banker; "Jackson has always paid his debts. If you can get him to sign your paper, we will loan you the money."

After Jackson found himself so deeply involved,

he resigned his judgeship to become a planter. Soon his cotton, corn, and tobacco throve greatly, and his horses were the fattest and his slaves the most industrious in the state.

Those were happy days for Andrew Jackson and his wife. They called their cabin the "Hermitage." At first there were only three rooms in the Hermitage, yet everybody was made welcome, from the peddler with his pack to the governor who came in his coach.

And here in 1805 came Aaron Burr. He had killed Alexander Hamilton in a duel, and was very unpopular in the states east of the mountains ; but he was well received by the people of Tennessee. They remembered how he had helped the territory to become a state.

Jackson remembered how kindly he had treated him in Philadelphia, and he invited him to his home.

And so Burr, the wanderer, spent many days at the Hermitage. He talked much about the conquest of Mexico.

Mexico was then a vast territory belonging to Spain. Besides the present boundary, it included what is now Texas, Arizona, New Mexico, Utah, California, and parts of Colorado and Kansas.

Jackson was still major-general of the Tennessee militia, and he pledged himself to build boats and equip men for the expedition.

After Burr had gone, reports came that he was plotting not only to conquer Mexico, but to make himself emperor over all the states west of the Alleghany Mountains.

These reports displeased Jackson very much. He wrote to some one, "I would die in the last ditch before I would see the Union disunited."

And when Burr came again to Clover Bottom, Jackson told him plainly enough that he would not lend aid to divide the Union. Burr declared that he had no intention of separating the West from the East.

Jackson believed him; and when President Jefferson ordered the arrest of Aaron Burr on the charge of treason to the United States, he hastened to Richmond, Virginia, to defend his friend at court.

We shall find that all through his life Andrew Jackson dared to do what he thought was right, and never deserted a friend in his hour of need.

VIII.—" OLD HICKORY."

Even after Kentucky, Tennessee, and Ohio
became states, the settlers west of the Alleghanies
lived in fear of the Indians.

The dusky warriors crept through the forests to
shoot at farmers who plowed in the fields, or hunters who followed their game; but they could not
keep peace among themselves long enough to unite
in a war against the white men. At last, Tecumseh, a Shawnee chief, wandered alone in the forest.
He was continually planning how to drive the palefaces away from the hunting-grounds. He decided
to unite all the Indian nations into one great army,
and he stirred up the tribes north of the Ohio until
they sharpened their tomahawks and danced together around the red pole of war.

Then he paddled across the beautiful river and
visited the Creeks, of Alabama. He chided them
for following the customs of the white men which
made the once noble warriors so weak.

" Lay aside the soft blankets of wool," he said,
" and don the skins of the forest.

"The Great Father is angry when he hears the
noise from your muskets. Put away the thunder

of the white men and take up again the bow and the hatchet."

While Tecumseh was thus busy in the South, his warriors in the North were defeated by General William Henry Harrison in the battle of Tippecanoe; and when the chief returned to find them scattered and slain, he fled to the British in Canada.

Now, the British were very unfriendly to the Americans. They insulted the Stars and Stripes on the ocean, and seized American sailors on board of American ships.

And when the British officers became so bold that they steered their men-of-war into our own harbors to seize our ships as prizes, President Madison declared war against Great Britain.

This was on the 19th of June, 1812. There were battles on land and on sea.

At first the Americans had the worst of it. The great fort at Detroit, on Lake Michigan, surrendered, and almost everything went wrong, until Captain Oliver H. Perry cleared Lake Erie of British ships.

Then General William Henry Harrison defeated

a British army on the Thames River, in Canada.
Tecumseh was slain in this battle, and many Indian
warriors deserted from the British.

Meantime, General Jackson, of Tennessee, was
not idle. He offered to bring two thousand five
hundred volunteers into the field, and his offer was
accepted. The troops were ordered South. It
seemed very important to guard the Gulf of Mexico. If New Orleans were seized by the British,
the whole valley of the Mississippi might be
lost.

Florida at that time belonged to Spain. The
Spanish king hoped that, if England might con-
quer the United States, the country west of the
Alleghanies would be annexed to Florida.

Spain claimed to be neutral, but allowed the
British to use Florida as a base of supplies, and
aided them by drilling the Indians and giving them
muskets of English make.

Jackson wrote to the secretary of war that he
could conquer Florida and plant the American
eagle on the walls of Pensacola and St. Augustine;
and he made everything ready for a long campaign
on the Gulf of Mexico.

It was midwinter when the general and his men boarded their boats on the Cumberland River. They paddled down the Ohio to the Mississippi, and it took them a month to pass through the ice to Natchez. Here Jackson spent another month waiting for orders from Washington. He kept the men hopeful by his ardor.

Once, when they seemed discouraged at the delay, he asked: "Where is the man that would not prefer to be buried in the ruins of his country than to live the slave of lords and tyrants?"

And when, at last, the orders came, they said to dismiss his troops, as it did not appear that the British would go South.

Jackson was greatly grieved over the result of his expedition, but he marched his men home through more than five hundred miles of forests and prairies. He gave up his three horses to carry the sick and walked like a common soldier.

He kept such stout courage that one man called him "tough," another called him "as tough as hickory," and then in gratitude they called him "Old Hickory," and the name of "Old Hickory" clung to him till the day of his death.

IX.—THE CREEK WAR.

If Jackson was not needed at New Orleans, he was needed to defend his country somewhere else.

The Creeks in the South could not forget the warnings of Tecumseh. They met in council, and pondered how they might drive out the white men. When an earthquake shook their wigwams, they said, "Tecumseh is stamping his foot in anger;" and when a meteor shot across the sky, they said, "It is the soul of Tecumseh, which can not rest till the palefaces are driven from the hunting-grounds."

The British officers at Pensacola offered five dollars apiece for American scalps, and the zeal of the warriors increased. Soon the settlements on the frontiers of Georgia and Tennessee were attacked, and the whites abandoned their farms and fled to the forts.

"We will carry war into the heart of their country," said General Jackson, of the Tennessee militia, and his men marched again to the South.

On one of the first battlefields an Indian baby was found clinging to its dead mother. The squaws in camp said, "Kill the papoose, for all of its kin are dead."

But General Jackson took the child to his own tent. He mixed brown sugar with water and kept it alive until it could be sent to the Hermitage.

Here the Indian baby found a home, and was loved like a son until he died at the age of seventeen.

There were many battles in this campaign against the Creeks. The Indians were driven step by step into their hiding places.

At last, Jackson halted on the banks of the Coosa and waited for supplies. No supplies came, because the rivers were then too shallow to float the boats.

There was soon nothing to eat but acorns and bark from the trees. It is said that one morning the general invited his officers to breakfast with him in his tent. Although starving themselves, they supposed that he had plenty to eat. When the proper hour arrived, a tray of acorns and a pitcher of water were brought in.

"Sit down, gentlemen," said Jackson; "this is my breakfast; but a soldier never despairs. Heaven will preserve us from famine and return us home *conquerors.*"

The days of fasting continued until the Tennesseeans declared they were ready to fight, but not to starve, and began to pack up to go home. All that General Jackson said had little effect.

When the militia started on their homeward march, Jackson called on the volunteers to help stop them. But very soon the volunteers themselves revolted, and then Jackson turned the guns of the militia against the volunteers.

Things continued to grow worse and worse, until Jackson promised that if no supplies came within two days he would break up the camp. The two days passed by, but not a bite of anything was in sight. The soldiers demanded that he should keep his promise.

"If only two will remain with me," said the general, "I will never abandon the fort;" and his face showed such anguish that more than a hundred rallied about him to pledge their support.

Most of the men started homeward. They soon met the long train of provisions, and with shouts of joy new camp fires were built and oxen were killed. The woods rang with merriment, while the soldiers feasted and drank.

Then with strength came boldness. The men declared that, now their legs were strong enough, they would go home in spite of Jackson. But they had hardly started before the fiery general was in their path.

There he stood. His face was pale, his eyes blazed like balls of fire, his gray hair rose straight up, as he cried in tones that echoed through the woods that he would shoot the first man who moved a step forward. The soldiers fled in a panic before him and returned to their tents.

Soon more recruits came, and the Indian war commenced again. "Until all is done, nothing is done," said Jackson.

He invaded the Holy Ground on the Talla-poosa, where the Indians declared no white man might enter and live, and prophets were slain, and warriors, squaws, and papooses perished. When the chiefs begged for peace, the army dis-banded.

Soon after this, the Creeks met at Fort Jackson

in the Holy Ground, to make a treaty. Jackson sat in a great circle of warriors.

"I have done the white people all the harm I could," said a chief; "and if I had an army, I would yet fight, but I have none. Once I could arouse my warriors, but I cannot arouse the dead. My warriors can no longer hear my voice. Their bones lie bleaching on the battlefields. You are a brave man, Jackson. I rely on your generosity."

Then another spoke: "A warrior went to the British on the lakes," he said; "when he returned, he brought gifts which made our warriors murder the Americans. Then the British at Pensacola misled the warriors.

"When you had your first war against the British we were young and foolish, and fought against you; but Father Washington warned us never to interfere between the British and the Americans. Now, if ever the British say we must fight again I will tell them no."

The most of the warriors agreed that their rivers might be navigated and that roads might be opened out through their country.

X.—THE BATTLE OF NEW ORLEANS.

While General Jackson was fighting the Indians, the fleets of Great Britain had been bringing more troops to America. A British army burned Washington, and President Madison and his Cabinet fled from the city.

People began to say that the British would soon place troops in every town and keep them there until the Americans swore allegiance to the king.

But you may be sure that Andrew Jackson never said such a thing as that. When a fleet sailed round the reefs of Florida and landed troops at Pensacola, he marched against Pensacola.

The Spaniards surrendered, the British withdrew to their ships, and the Indians scattered through the forest.

Then Jackson set out for New Orleans, in Louisiana, a hundred and seventy miles away.

Now, Louisiana had just been admitted to the Union. The people of the new state were mostly Spanish, French, and negroes.

New Orleans, its capital, was different from any other city in the United States. It was fortified by an old wall, with bastions at four corners where sentinels always stood. And there was a great cathedral, and a curious town hall; and there were houses with arcades, lattices, and balconies. On the levees by the Mississippi River were piles of cotton bales, and casks of sugar and molasses, waiting to be shipped to the West Indies.

As Jackson entered the city, he marked well these piles of casks and bales, and made up his mind just what to do with them. He said that they should help him in the fight.

The people of New Orleans hailed his approach with delight. " Jackson's come! Jackson's come!" went from lip to lip in Spanish, French, and English, and " Yankee Doodle" was sung on the streets by singers who could not pronounce the words.

Now, the people of this strange city had looked for a grand general with a mustache and epaulettes and a staff of officers in splendid uniforms.

They saw a tall, thin man, dressed in threadbare clothes, with a short, blue cloak, and boots reaching to the knee, and with him were five or six others as poorly dressed as himself.

Jackson soon showed that he was every inch a

general. He did not rest a moment. He declared
martial law. He gave orders that all street lamps
should be put out at nine o'clock, and that no one
should enter or leave the city without passports
from headquarters. He appealed to the French,
Spanish, free negroes, and Americans to defend
their state from the redcoats.

He even called on the smugglers for aid. There
was old Jean Lafitte, who had an island in the Gulf
where he hid the rich booty he seized. Jackson
promised pardon for his smuggling, and soon the
ships of the sea robbers lay in wait for the British
fleet.

Jackson summoned the engineers to examine
the bayous and harbors, and hundreds of men
were set to digging ditches and carrying dirt
in wheelbarrows, shovels, and carts. Bales of
cotton and hogsheads of sugar were heaped into
line.

One rich dealer in cotton called to Jackson:
"You must appoint a guard for this cotton of
mine."

"Certainly," replied Jackson. "Here, sergeant,
give this gentleman a musket and ammunition and

station him in the line of defence. No man is
better qualified to guard cotton than the man who
owns it!"

There were plenty of volunteers. The young
aristocrats of the city became aids-de-camp;
regiments in flatboats came down from Nashville;
friendly Indians gathered in feathers and war
paint, and soon five thousand men were toiling
day and night on the breastworks.

"There'll be time enough for sleep when we've
driven the villains into the swamp," said Jackson.
The army was still at work on the twenty-fourth
of December.

Now, at that very time, in the town of Ghent
across the sea, a treaty of peace was being signed
between the agents of Great Britain and those
of the United States; but there was no ocean cable
then to carry this news to America.

No one in the United States expected peace yet,
and the eyes of all were turned toward the army
at New Orleans. President Madison and his
cabinet, the senators, and members of the House
of Representatives at Washington waited eagerly
for news. One naval officer studied the map of

New Orleans, and said it could not be defended against a fleet of fifty vessels, armed with a thousand cannon.

Twenty thousand British soldiers were confident of success. They were the flower of England's army and navy; many of them had fought against Napoleon, and some of their ships had been in great victories on the Nile River, in Egypt.

"I shall eat my Christmas dinner in New Orleans," said the British admiral.

"Perhaps so," said General Jackson when he heard of it, "but I shall have the honor of presiding at that dinner!"

Ladies sent a message to ask what they should do if the city were attacked. "Say to them," said the general, "not to be uneasy. No British soldier shall enter New Orleans as an enemy unless over my dead body."

At last, the British in red, and green, and tartan plaids marched toward the earthworks.

Perhaps at that very moment General Jackson remembered the British officer who had struck him across the head because he would not black his boots, and perhaps he remembered how his two brothers and his mother had died in the first war with the redcoats.

His cannon belched fire from the wall in front of him, and a score of British officers fell. A retreat was sounded.

Then on the eighth day of January, the soldiers of King George advanced again. On they came and their cannon balls whistled a greeting.

"Don't mind those rockets," said Jackson; "they are mere toys to amuse children !"

"Old Hickory" seemed to be everywhere at one time. "Stand to your guns!" he cried to one. "See that every shot tells!" he called to another.

In twenty-five minutes the victory was won, but it had been an awful battle for the British. More than two thousand of them were killed and wounded.

Only eight of Jackson's men were killed and thirteen wounded. And when the guns ceased firing, and the sentinels called down from the watchtowers of New Orleans that the redcoats had fled to their ships, songs of praise rang out from the cathedral, and the people flocked into the streets to welcome the return of the conqueror.

Now, all this time rumors good and bad had reached the cities east of the mountains. Snow storms delayed the couriers, and when, at last, the news of victory came, people could hardly believe it.

"And who *is* Jackson?" they cried. But it was not long till all the newspapers had plenty to say about Andrew Jackson of Clover Bottom, in Tennessee; and Congress gave him a vote of thanks and ordered a gold medal in his honor.

When the tardy report of the Treaty of Ghent arrived, Federalists and Republicans, who had not spoken for years, clasped hands like old friends. There were bonfires and wild huzzas, and long lines of sleighs drove through the streets of many towns with " Peace " on the hatbands of the drivers.

"Hurrah for Jackson!" called the merry-makers as they passed each other with jingling bells.

During all the year the merchant vessels had lain idle in the harbors with tar barrels over the masts to protect them. "Madison's nightcaps," the barrels had been called; and now that commerce was safe again, thousands flocked down to the wharves to see Madison's nightcaps lifted off as the ships sailed away to foreign ports.

The Union was stronger than ever. Every one
had fought for it, or paid for it, or wept for it in
this war of 1812. But Andrew Jackson received
more honor than any other man. One poet wrote:
" A happy New Year for Columbia begun
    When our Jackson secured what our Washington won."

XI.—GOVERNOR OF FLORIDA.

After a few months' rest at the Hermitage, the
hero of New Orleans went on horseback through
the Cumberland Gap toward Washington, and all
along his pathway people turned out to greet him.

In Virginia, Thomas Jefferson, now very old,
offered a toast in his honor. At Washington, he
became the idol of the hour. His stateliness won
the hearts of the ladies, and his cordial manner
pleased the men. He was made a major-general
of the United States army, and had riches, honor,
and fame.

He returned home, but he did not remain there
long. "In time of peace prepare for war," said
Jackson. He posted troops at New Orleans, and

held council fires with the Indians to settle disputes about land.

Then some negroes began to give trouble. Many slaves from Georgia had escaped from their masters to northern Florida. They gathered herds and flocks, and built homes, and called themselves free. They numbered nearly a thousand, and had chiefs and captains, who drilled them at arms.

After a time they seized a fort on the Appalachicola River, and began to plunder the Americans. The fort was in Florida, but, because the Spaniards did not have troops to attack it, some of Jackson's troops blew it up.

Then the Seminoles in Georgia and Alabama grew restless. They welcomed the fleeing negroes to their wigwams and raised the red pole of war as they sang of the white scalps they would take. General Jackson marched from Nashville with an army and scattered the warriors.

And when he saw that the Spaniards were aiding the Indians, he seized the fort of St. Marks, in Florida, drove out the Spanish garrison, hauled down the Spanish flag, and put in its place the Stars and Stripes.

In a few months he had broken the power of the Seminoles completely and had not lost a single man. But what about the seizure of the Spanish fort? Spain was at peace with the United States. The boldness of "Old Hickory" might bring on a war with the Spanish king. Some said that Congress, to avoid a war, should pass a vote of censure on General Jackson.

The hero was too popular with the people for this to be done, but the American troops were withdrawn from the Spanish fort.

Now, the Spanish king knew very well that he could not continue to hold Florida without the aid of a large army; and so when President Monroe soon afterwards proposed to buy the province, he sold it for five million dollars. Jackson was appointed the first governor of Florida.

In those days Florida was a wilderness of swamps and live oaks, with here and there a half-ruined fort. On the east coast was St. Augustine, the oldest town in the United States, and on the west was Pensacola, where the Spanish governor lived.

Governor Jackson marched into Pensacola with

a regiment, and the Spanish flag on the government building was taken down. The Spaniards, whose lands had been sold by the king, crowded the harbor with their household goods, and set sail for Cuba in a fleet of ships.

American adventurers hastened to buy up land for speculation, and drowsy old Pensacola soon had the appearance of a brisk American town.

Governor Jackson remained only a few months in Florida. The climate did not agree with him, and he resigned his office to return to the Hermitage. He was welcomed home with great joy by the people of Nashville. They felt that his honors were their honors, and were proud of him wherever he went.

When President Monroe visited Nashville, a ball was given in his honor; but the ornament of the ball seemed to be the general rather than the president. The two men marched into the hall arm in arm. General Jackson was much taller than President Monroe, and was dressed in full uniform.

"Ah, see our general!" whispered the citizens; "he surpasses all in the room!"

XII.—The Hermitage.

And so it was in Clover Bottom that Andrew Jackson again found himself at home. The Hermitage was now a comfortable brick house with wide piazzas where rich and poor were welcomed alike.

Jackson often drove to Nashville in a carriage drawn by four handsome iron-gray horses, with black servants in liveries ; and as he wound in and out among hay wagons and strings of mules that blocked up the streets, the simple country people in the market place thought him a very grand person indeed. Yet when General Lafayette stopped at the Hermitage in 1825, he was surprised at the plain living of the hero of New Orleans.

"What!" exclaimed one of the Frenchmen who accompanied him, "what! Does the most famous general in America live thus? In France he would have a palace in the city and a country seat, and his houses would be filled with liveried servants and costly silver and gold plate, and all France would be taxed to pay for his splendor!"

But the more the old marquis knew General Jackson, the more he admired him; and after he had bidden him adieu, he said to some of his

friends: "That is a great man. He has much before him yet!"

Now, it had been nearly forty years since Andrew Jackson first crossed the mountains, and wonderful changes had taken place in the West. After steamboats were invented, thousands of settlers came down the Ohio every year. Towns sprang up along the rivers; forests and prairies were made into fine farms, and schoolhouses and churches were everywhere.

So many states had been admitted into the Union that the people of the great West began to say: "Why can't we send a President to Washington? Here we are, Kentucky, Tennessee, Ohio, Louisiana, Indiana, Illinois, Alabama, and Missouri, and we have boundless territory from which to make more states. We have conquered the Indians, and driven out the wild beasts, and cut down the forests; we have sent our best men to the north to defeat the British and to the south to defeat them. We have earned a high place in the nation. Let us put on a bold front and demand the highest place. Let us ask that a man from the West shall be made President."

Ah, but who could win in an election against a candidate from the East?

"Who, indeed," cried Tennessee—"who *could* win but the hero of New Orleans? Who but 'Old Hickory' is known to the people on the coast?"

And so the Tennessee legislature nominated Andrew Jackson for President of the United States.

Now, just across the border was the Kentucky legislature, whose hero was Henry Clay.

"The President from the West must not be the laughing stock of scholars and statesmen," said Kentucky. "Jackson is brave, but he is ignorant. Let us name Henry Clay. He is a polished statesman. We shall never be ashamed of Harry of the West."

And so Henry Clay was nominated by his friends in Kentucky.

But the politicians of the East did not want a man from the West. They nominated John Quincy Adams and other Eastern men for the office.

Jackson himself laughed at the idea of being President. "No, I can command a body of troops in a rough way," he said, "but I am not fit to be President."

Who would be President? That was the question on the lips of all. The choice seemed to lie between Jackson and Adams.

Would it be the Western planter, the Indian fighter, the stern soldier of 1812, or would it be the elegant scholar who had spent years at the courts of kings?

The friends of Jackson hurrahed for "Old Hickory." They called him a second Washington, and it looked for a time as though he would surely be elected.

Daniel Webster wrote to his brother Ezekiel: "General Jackson's manners are more presidential than those of any of the candidates. He is grave and mild. My wife is for him decidedly."

In the end, John Quincy Adams was elected.

But the West was determined to name the next President, and the man it wanted was Andrew Jackson. Four years later, he was elected by a great vote of the people both in the East and in the West.

XIII.—President of the United States.

Soon after General Jackson was elected President, his wife died. He was broken-hearted over his loss, for she had been a kind and loving wife. He wished to remain at the Hermitage, where he might be near her grave; but the people had called him to office, and he felt that he must serve them.

He took a steamboat down the Cumberland and up the Ohio to Pittsburg, and then rode to Washington to be inaugurated on the 4th of March, 1829, as the seventh President of the United States.

There were six secretaries in the official cabinet; but he did not ask much advice from these. He sought out a few friends whom he consulted so much that they were called the "Kitchen Cabinet." When Congress passed bills he did not think were best for the country, he vetoed them. If Congress could not pass them again by a vote of two-thirds they failed to become laws.

There were many questions about which people differed very much in opinion, and one of these was the tariff question. A tariff is a tax laid on certain goods imported from foreign countries.

"Out with foreign wares!" cried the manu-facturing states of the North. "Put a high tariff on the manufactures from Europe, and give us a chance to make everything for ourselves!"

But the states of the South did not manufacture anything; they wanted to exchange their cotton, tobacco, rice, and indigo for the products of Europe, as cheaply as possible. They did not want to pay a tax on imported wares.

Now, President Jackson was opposed to the high tariff law. His friends in the South declared that he would have sympathy with them if they refused to allow the taxes to be collected at their ports by the government officers.

But Jackson said to himself: "This high tariff has now become a law of the land by a vote of the majority of the people; and since I was elected to execute this law, as well as all others, I am deter-mined to have it enforced."

The members of Congress from the South gave a great banquet, to which they invited President Jackson. He heard some of the guests say that, if

Congress would not change the tariff law, the states that did not like the law might withdraw from the Union.   What did that mean?

Jackson knew very well that it meant that our country should be divided into many little republics instead of being one great republic, as George Washington and others had intended when they signed the Constitution of the United States.

When the time came to make speeches, the President rose to offer a toast.   All leaned eagerly forward.   They thought he would say something against the tariff.

But the Man of the Iron Will looked down the long lines of brilliant men and exclaimed: "Our Federal Union, it *must* be preserved!"   These words caused much dismay among the guests. They saw that the President would oppose any attempt to secede from the Union.

After a time South Carolina grew bold, and declared that the state would secede if tariffs were collected at her ports, and ordered the militia to be ready to act if necessary.

President Jackson did not hesitate a moment.

He sent two war-ships to Charleston, and this quickly prevented a rebellion.

He lived according to the very words he had spoken when an unknown soldier in Tennessee: " I shall be found in the last extremity endeavoring to discharge the duty I owe to my country."

XIV.—Death at the Hermitage.

Andrew Jackson served eight years as President, and each year he grew more popular with the people.

In spite of all enemies, everything seemed to prosper during his administration.   The cotton crops in the South were enormous.   The wheat and corn in the middle and western states yielded more than the Americans could use, and shiploads of grain were sent to foreign lands.   The national debt was paid.   Steamboat lines, pike roads, railroads, and canals were built.

There were so many labor-saving machines invented that farmers and mechanics had more time to read, and some newspapers were sold for a penny apiece. American poets, historians, and orators began to be talked about in Europe. And all this progress added much to the glory of Andrew Jackson.

He put on a haughty air with the French, and forced them to pay a large amount of money for damage to our merchantmen during their wars.

He sent armies to Wisconsin and to Georgia to conquer the troublesome Indians; and when news came that the Seminoles were plotting again to massacre the white settlers, he sent troops who drove them into the swamps of Florida.

But, although Jackson fought the warriors when they were on the warpath, he wished to be just to them in times of peace.

The United States bought Indian lands, and he said: " Pay the Indians honorably for their lands— their full value in silver, not blankets, not rifles nor powder, but hard cash."

And he advised Congress to set apart an Indian territory west of the Mississippi, where all the tribes might seek a home and make laws for themselves.

While on a tour through New England, cannons

boomed at his approach, flags waved, and dinners were the order of the day; and when Jackson laid the corner stone of a monument to Mary, the mother of Washington, the patriotism of the people was raised to the highest pitch.

Harvard College made him a "Doctor of Laws."

"Why, Jackson can hardly write his own name," said his enemies, "and a Doctor of Laws is a title for scholars!"

A curious crowd looked on while a learned professor addressed the President in a long Latin speech. Everybody smiled. There sat "Old Hickory" on the platform, and people knew well enough that he did not understand a word that was said. When the Latin speech was over, a wag called out to Jackson for some Latin, and then everybody smiled again.

But the old hero rose politely, and, stepping forward, said, "*E Pluribus Unum.*" It was the motto put on the American seal by Benjamin Franklin. Every schoolboy knows it who has jingled quarters in his pocket—"One made out of many!"

Who did not remember at that moment how Jackson had preserved the many states as one united country when South Carolina tried to secede? And who did not remember how he had fought, over and over again, for the Union? Cheers rent the air for the new Doctor of Laws, and the greatest scholars in the college hastened to shake his hand.

At the close of his second term he said, in his farewell address, " I leave this great people prosperous and happy."

Jackson traveled homeward by easy stages. He was now seventy years old. He lived the life of a planter the rest of his life. He was respectful to women and loving and tender to children. Even his bitterest enemies said that he had been brave and skillful as a soldier and honest and fearless as a statesman.

Nobody visited Nashville without driving out to the Hermitage to visit " The General."

In his house were many interesting relics. Not the least of these was a blue and yellow uniform worn by the hero at New Orleans, which you may see to-day in the Patent Office at Washington.

During the week, Jackson was always ready to ride or walk with his guests, but on Sundays he would say: "Gentlemen, do what you please in my home; I am going to church."

And on one Sunday in June the soul of the fearless man took its flight. He was surrounded by his family and servants and a few of his dearest friends. His last words were:

" Be good, my dear children and friends and servants. I hope to meet you all in heaven, both white and black!"

He was buried by the side of his wife in the garden of the Hermitage, and the tablet which marks his grave reads:

GENERAL ANDREW JACKSON.

Born on the 15th of March, 1767.

Died on the 8th of June, 1845.

THE STORY OF

ULYSSES S. GRANT

ULYSSES S. GRANT.

THE STORY OF ULYSSES S. GRANT.

I.—NAMING THE BABY.

Jesse Root Grant was a young tanner who lived in Clermont County, Ohio. It is said that his ancestors belonged to a Scottish clan whose motto was: "Stand fast, stand firm, stand sure."

His great-grandfather, "honest Matthew" Grant, landed on Nantasket Beach, in Massachusetts, in 1630, just ten years after the Pilgrims landed on Plymouth Rock. His grandfather was a soldier in the French and Indian war, and his father was a lieutenant in the Revolution.

Jesse Grant was proud of his ancestors. He tried to honor their memory by his own upright life and often said that "Stand fast, stand firm, stand sure" was just as good a motto for an American as for a Scotchman.

He was so honest and industrious that he was respected by all who knew him.

After he had saved enough money to build a house he married pretty Hannah Simpson. Their new home was at Point Pleasant near the Ohio

River. The country around them was rough and wild, and Indians prowled in the forests, but they did not seem to mind that.

Young Grant whitewashed his cottage inside and out; he planted seeds for vines at the doorway and made a gravel walk to the gate.

Hannah wove mats for the floor and put curtains at the windows and hung all her new bright tins on the wall.

They were very happy; and on the 27th of April, 1822, the first baby came. It was a great event for the whole neighborhood.

"A boy, is it?" said one. "Well, if he's a second Jesse he'll be a blessing to Clermont County."

"Aye, and to the state, and to the United States," said another.

Many names were proposed for the new comer, but the doting parents were not satisfied with any of them.

The weeks went by. "Hello, Baby!" said Jesse, when he entered the house. "Bye-bye, Baby!" he called when he went away.

One day Hannah said: "It will never do. See what a big boy he is already. He must have a name. Let us drive over to father's and ask him about it."

And so when baby Grant was a month old he was bundled up and taken to Grandfather Simpson's in search of a name.

Grandfather and grandmother and two aunts were at the door to receive him. How proud the old folks were when they looked into the round, blue eyes of their first grandchild! And how the aunts laughed and chattered as they took off his shawls and showed his pink little hands and feet.

"What is his name?" they all cried in a breath.

"Well," said Hannah, "Jesse wants one name and I want another, and you shall decide. Which shall it be, Albert, after Albert Gallatin, the statesman of Pennsylvania, or Ulysses, after the hero of the Greeks?"

"Neither, daughter, neither," said Grandfather Simpson. "The name above all is Hiram, that of the king whom Solomon loved."

"Oh no!" cried one of the aunts, "Theodore is so much prettier than either of the others."

"Well, well," said Grandfather Simpson; "let us ballot for the name. Bring pen, ink and paper and

write what you like on a slip. We will then put
the ballots into a hat and shake them, and the one
first picked out shall be the name."

The smiling old farmer held out the hat and all
the votes went in. Little did he think that ballots
would ever make his grandchild president of the
United States!

The hat was shaken with a will. A slip was
taken out: "Ulysses!" said Hannah, "its just what
I wanted."

But the grandfather looked so disappointed that
the child was called Hiram Ulysses. Now Hiram
was a wise and upright ruler, and Ulysses was a
warrior who fought for his country and then
traveled over the whole known world.

I am sure that when you have read about Hiram
Ulysses Grant you will say that he resembled his
namesakes very much.

II.—The Home in Georgetown.

When Ulysses was nearly a year old, Mr. Grant
moved to Georgetown, a little village about forty
miles east of Cincinnati.

He built a house near a creek which emptied into the Ohio river, and established a tannery to make skins into leather.

Ulysses grew very fast and was petted by everybody. One day, when he was two years old, there was a celebration of some kind in Georgetown. Perhaps it was because John Quincy Adams had just been elected President of the United States. Many people were on the streets. Jesse Grant held Ulysses high up in his arms to see the procession.

"Hello, Lyss!" said a boy with a pistol. "Want to shoot? Let him fire it, Mr. Grant."

The father put the baby fingers to the trigger. Bang! went the pistol. The women screamed; but Ulysses did not wink or dodge.

"Fick it again! Fick it again!" he shouted in glee, and again the report rang out.

"He'll make a general, sure," said a bystander.

Ulysses often played in the tan bark near the mill. He saw trading flat-boats float down the Ohio river loaded with apples, cider, and corn; and family barges carrying settlers farther west; and sometimes a steamer passed by, with loud whistles and a great deal of smoke.

When he was older he ground tan bark for his father by driving in a circle a horse hitched to the bark-mill. He learned to swim and dive in a deep hole in the creek. He skated, and trapped rabbits in winter; and he amused himself all the year round much as other boys do.

He was not very brilliant at school. He was shy and slow, but because he was diligent he almost always succeeded in what he attempted to do.

" Believe that you can and you can," said Ulysses.

He would not lie. His honest blue eyes looked straight into the eyes of his playmates and they believed whatever he said.

He sometimes brought his friends home with him to spend the night. They would gather about the kitchen hearth, where the fire blazed high, and play checkers, or tell riddles while they ate apples or cracked hickory nuts, and after a game of fox-and-geese they went to bed in the loft overhead.

The first book that Ulysses read through was a Life of George Washington. Once he came near being punished because he defended the name of Washington. It came about in this way: His cousin John, who lived in Canada, made him a visit. Because Canada belonged to England, John was loyal to his king. He thought the United States should be an English province.

He said to Ulysses: " Your boasted Washington was a traitor when he fought against King George."

" You say that again and I'll thrash you," shouted Ulysses.

" I do say it again," said the little Canadian.

Both boys had pluck. Coats were off and the battle waxed fierce between the American eagle and the British lion.

In the end John lay sprawling on the ground. When Ulysses went into the house his mother saw that he had been in a fight. She made ready to punish him with a birch rod.

But his father said: "I do not think you ought to whip him. He has never quarreled with his cousin before. He fought in defense of his country, and he *ought* to defend his country." And so the boy escaped punishment.

From the time he could walk, Ulysses showed great love for horses. When he was about seven years old he climbed to the manger, put a collar and harness on a young colt, and then made the animal haul brushwood all day long.

At ten he drove with some leather from George-town to Cincinnati, and brought passengers back with him. He would ride bareback standing on one foot while his horse ran at full speed.

Once there was much excitement about a tricky pony that came to town. It was said to go round a ring like lightning and throw anyone who tried to ride it. Ulysses sat among the boys as the pony was led out.

"Will some one step up and ride this pony?" asked the jockey, smiling and bowing.

Ulysses mounted the pony. It began to kick and plunge; and when the little rider kept his seat it ran round the ring at full speed. Then out jumped a monkey and sprang on the boy's shoulder and pulled his hair, while the pony ran faster than ever. Ulysses sat bolt upright.

He did not smile nor look to the right or the left. The monkey chattered; the pony drooped its ears; and everybody laughed as the mortified jockey led them away.

III.—THE WEST POINT CADET.

One day when Ulysses was busy in the tannery his father said: "My son, I believe you are going to receive the appointment."

"What appointment, father?"

"To West Point. I have applied for it."

Ulysses knew that a boy had just failed in the examination at West Point. He was afraid lest he also would fail, and so he said: "I don't want to go, father."

"But I wish it," said his father.

"Well, then, I suppose I shall go," he replied. He studied hard to prepare for the examination.

The people of Georgetown could scarcely believe that Lyss Grant was going to West Point. They looked upon him as a dull boy who cared only for horses, and they laughed at the idea of his wearing brass buttons and shoulder straps.

In 1839, when he was just seventeen years old, Ulysses set out for Ripley, which was the landing for the steamboat bound for Pittsburg.

He wore a new suit of clothes and had a hundred dollars in his pocket; but, for all that, his courage was at a low ebb. If he failed in examination he would only be making the long journey to bring disgrace on his family.

When he reached Pittsburg he took the canal boat to Harrisburg ; then he rode in a railroad car to Philadelphia. The train traveled at the rate of twelve miles an hour, which seemed to be wonderfully fast.

At Philadelphia he called on his aunts. They made much of him and showed him about the Quaker City. He visited Carpenters' Hall where the first Continental Congress had met, and Federal Hall where President Washington had delivered his famous farewell address before Congress, and where John Adams had been inaugurated the second president of the United States. He went to the graveyard on Arch street where Benjamin Franklin lay buried, and he saw the old Penn mansion where Benedict Arnold, who became a traitor to his country, once lived with his beautiful Tory wife.

Ulysses wished he might stay longer in Philadelphia ; but he was obliged to say good-bye to his kind aunts. He was soon in New York City.

And then one bright May morning he stepped

on a steamboat and was carried up the Hudson
River. When someone at his elbow said that the
low buildings on the left bank were the West Point
barracks his heart sank within him. He dreaded
the examination very much.

At last the trial was over. Young Grant was
found to be sound in body and more than five feet
high and he answered enough questions for admission to West Point.

This meant that he could enter one of the best
schools in the country. The United States government would pay him for learning to be a
trained soldier and a polished gentleman ; and
when he had finished his studies he would receive
a commission in the regular army.

Hiram Ulysses Grant was enrolled as Ulysses
Simpson Grant through a mistake of the congressman who appointed him to the position. Ulysses
tried to have the name changed ; but he was called
Ulysses Simpson the rest of his life.

Most of the cadets received nicknames. One
was called "Dad" because his hair was turning gray;
another "Doc" because he had clerked in a drug
store ; another "Chub" because he was stout.

Ulysses was called " Uncle Sam " because his initials were "U. S."

He was, at first, put into the awkward squad, and a few snobs called him " mudsill " when they saw how awkward he was.

But he had no false pride to be hurt ; and he was always so modest and manly that he soon won the respect of all.

There was much to do at West Point. The drum beat at five o'clock in the morning and the infantry drilled five days in the week. The lessons were long and difficult. There were maps of battlefields to draw, bridges to make, forts to build and intrenchments to fortify. There was engineering practice and artillery and cavalry drill.

Ulysses was the most daring rider in his class. "Old York" was a famous horse in camp which only one other besides himself dared to mount.

When seated on Old York he cleared a fence six feet and three inches high, which was the most noted leap ever made in the school.

Grant was four years at West Point. He marched in review before President Martin Van Buren ; but whenever he saw General Winfield

Scott ride about the drill ground on his splendid horse he thought he would rather be a general than a president.

When Grant was graduated he received a commission as lieutenant of the 4th infantry regiment of Ohio.

He returned home for a vacation before going to camp with the regular army. His friends in Georgetown found him much changed. He was taller and straighter, and his dress was always neat.

At first he took pride in wearing his full uniform; but one day his pride had a fall. As he was returning home from a stroll, in fine humor with himself he saw a drunken stable boy parading in front of his house. The fellow's ragged shirt was adorned with brass buttons and his nankeen pantaloons had a white stripe sewed down the seams. He wore neither hat nor shoes; but he held his head very high and marched up and down with the stately step of the new lieutenant, while street urchins cheered him on.

This parade taught Grant a lesson, and he resolved to wear his uniform only when duty required it.

IV.—The Mexican War.

Lieutenant Grant began military service for the United States in 1843. The standing army numbered about ten thousand men. The troops were scattered in small squads about the country; for we were at peace with all the world except the Indians.

Grant was sent with the 4th infantry regiment to Missouri. He went on duty at Jefferson barracks, near St. Louis. The Indians did not make much trouble, and camp life was dull; but he spent many pleasant evenings in St. Louis at the home of the Dents.

Pretty little Julia Dent was the sister of his West Point roommate, and Grant soon became her devoted admirer.

It was not long before there was much talk about the new state of Texas. Texas had once been a part of Mexico. When Santa Anna became president of that republic he was so unpopular that the Texans refused to live under his rule. They set up a republic of their own with Samuel Houston, an American, as president.

Then Santa Anna marched his army across the

Rio Grande River to conquer the rebellious province; but he was forced to march back again.

France, England, and the United States acknowledged the independence of Texas. Most of the citizens in that country were Americans, and they soon asked that their state might be annexed to the United States.

The people of the South wanted Texas admitted to the Union. It was a fine cotton country, it had a long sea coast for shipping to foreign ports, and it might be divided into several slave states.

But the people of the North bitterly opposed the admission of Texas because they did not wish slavery extended.

At last near the close of President John Tyler's administration Texas was admitted. The new state soon caused trouble. A dispute arose about the southern boundary line. The Mexicans claimed that it was on the river Nueces, but the Texans said that it extended farther south to the Rio Grande.

President James K. Polk took the side of Texas in the quarrel and, in 1846, he sent General

Zachary Taylor with an army to the disputed territory.

Lieutenant Grant and his regiment hastened to join General Taylor.

The Mexican troops crossed the Rio Grande and attacked the Americans. General Taylor drove them back across the river.

Grant's company guarded the artillery; the young lieutenant proved so useful that he was made quartermaster to look after supplies.

General Taylor soon marched against Monterey. This was the largest city in northern Mexico. It lay in the midst of beautiful orchards and vineyards, and was guarded by ten thousand Mexican soldiers.

While the battle was raging the ammunition in Grant's regiment gave out. Someone must order more. The headquarters were four miles away on the other side of the camp. To reach them a courier must ride straight through the enemy's city.

Grant volunteered to go on the dangerous errand. He mounted a swift horse, hung one foot over the saddle and, catching hold by the mane, started off like a Comanche Indian. Away the horse flew through the streets of Monterey, while muskets were being fired from all the windows. Neither horse nor rider was hurt, and Grant soon returned with a wagon load of ammunition.

Monterey was captured, and then Grant's regiment was sent to the mouth of the Rio Grande to join General Winfield Scott on his way to the City of Mexico.

General Scott landed with his army at Vera Cruz. The troops marched within sight of volcanoes crowned with snow, and past ruined temples and pyramids, built by the Aztec Indians long before the Spaniards discovered Mexico.

The army fought as it marched. The nearer it came to the capital the more it was opposed by the desperate enemy.

Grant was always in the thickest of the fight. He received promotion at Molino del Rey, or the Mill of the King. This was a long stone fortification where grain was stored. While the batteries were bombarding the strong wall, Grant and a few others forced a gate, climbed to a roof, and captured six Mexican officers and several privates.

The King's Mill was taken; but between it and Mexico stood a high mound called Chapultepec. Its rocky sides were bristling with guns. The mound was taken after a hard fight.

Grant, with a few volunteers, pulled a small cannon under an aqueduct, which carried water into Mexico. He crept along in the shadow of its pillars till he reached a church which overlooked the city. With his comrades he dragged the cannon up to the belfry and, opening fire, dislodged the enemy from an important position.

"That was a brilliant idea!" exclaimed the commanding officer, and he sent Lieutenant Pemberton to bring Grant to headquarters to receive his personal thanks.

This Lieutenant Pemberton, as we shall see, would one day be defeated by Grant on quite another field of battle.

Major Robert E. Lee made special mention of Grant in his report on Chapultepec. "Second Lieutenant Grant," he said "behaved with distinguished gallantry." Major Lee little thought that he would be defeated by Grant on many fields of battle.

Mexico surrendered. When General Scott entered the city Grant was at his side

The army went into camp while waiting for a treaty of peace to be signed. Grant was still quartermaster. The soldiers were ragged, and he set Mexican tailors to work on new uniforms. Provisions were almost gone and he rented a stone bakery, bought flour and fuel, and hired Mexican bakers to make bread.

He managed the funds of the regiment so well that he saved money enough to furnish a band of musicians and provide other luxuries.

You may be sure that he was popular with his men. Meanwhile he visited the places of interest in the quaint old city. He went to one of the bull fights, where horsemen, armed with long spears, tortured wild bulls to death; but the sight of such cruelty made him sick and he would not stay to watch it.

He climbed Mount Popocatepetl and was lost with some comrades, in a storm, for several hours. One of the party was Captain Buckner who would one day surrender an army to Grant. But, of course, neither of them ever thought of such a thing as that, and they had many a jaunt together among the ,ruins of old Mexico.

In 1848 the treaty of Guadalupe was signed. There was peace again between Mexico and the United States. Grant set sail with his regiment, and was soon home again.

He was just twenty-six years old. He had served under the best officers in the army; he had seen cities besieged and stout forts carried by storm, and he had become acquainted with most of the military men in the country.

The knowledge gained in the Mexican war was to be of great service to him later on.

V.—On the Pacific Coast.

Soon after Lieutenant Grant's return from the Mexican war he married Julia Dent of St. Louis. They lived wherever the 4th regiment was stationed, until 1852, when the regiment was ordered to California. Grant then told his young wife that she must remain at home. He said that the Pacific coast was so far off that she must not even expect a letter for several months. There was a sad parting when he set out on his journey.

Now before you could possibly guess why Grant's regiment was sent to the coast you must know what wonderful events had occurred since the treaty with Mexico.

By that treaty upper California, with a great deal of other land, was ceded to the United States.

California had good harbors and a fertile soil, but it was so far from the states that no one thought it would ever be very thickly settled.

Hardly was the treaty signed, however, when it was reported that gold had been discovered near the Sacramento River. The news spread round the world. San Francisco, a sleepy little Spanish mission with a few mud cabins, became a city of many thousands within a year.

Americans, Mexicans, Germans, Frenchmen, Englishmen, and Chinamen flocked into California and scattered over the gold fields.

Saloons and gambling-houses were every where. The reckless miners provoked the Indians to go on the warpath; and then helpless citizens called on the government for protection. And so it came about that Grant's regiment was ordered to California.

There was no railroad to the coast in those days. The journey across the prairies and over the mountains was so slow and so dangerous that the troops went by way of the Isthmus of Panama. They set sail at New York and landed at Aspinwall.

Now, today, a swift train of cars crosses the isthmus from Aspinwall to Panama City; but in 1852 there was no railroad, and it sometimes took weeks to make the journey.

The regiment began its slow march in the hot month of July. Poisonous vapors lurked in the marshes and a fever broke out. Grant was still quartermaster. He furnished food and fresh water; distributed medicines, and fought the plague as best he could. But more than fifty of his comrades died.

When the survivors of the 4th regiment reached California they went into camp near San Francisco. They helped restore order among the miners, and scattered the Indians to their wigwams.

Then Grant's company was stationed at Vancouver, at that time in Oregon Territory. People in the East were emigrating more and more to the West. It was said that a railroad ought to be built to the coast, and several surveying parties were sent out by the government to examine the different routes.

In 1853 Lieutenant George B. McClellan came to Vancouver with some engineers to make a survey for a Northern Pacific railroad.

Grant had been with McClellan in the Mexican war, and was delighted to meet him again. He lodged him in his best tent, and gave him his fleetest horse to ride. Grant was a fine host. When his army friends gathered about him none described the Mexican campaign so well as he.

After one of the talks an officer said: "How clear headed Grant is in describing a battle! He seems to see the whole thing."

But in all the talks around the camp fire he never said anything he would be ashamed for his mother to hear. When an officer was about to repeat a story, and said, as he looked around: "There are no ladies here—."

" No," said Grant, "but there are *gentlemen!* " and the bad story was never told.

After a time Lieutenant Grant was made captain of a company in California. But camp life on the frontier was dull; the pay was not enough to support his family on the coast, where everything was very expensive, and he felt that he could not always be separated from his loved ones.

And so, in 1854, Captain Grant resigned his commission in the army. He said to a friend, as he started for home, " Whoever hears from me in ten years will probably hear of a well-to-do Missouri farmer."

VI.—Farmer and Leather Merchant.

When Grant landed in New York he was obliged to send to his father for money to get home. He was thirty-two years old. He knew no profession except that of the army, and he had a wife and children to support.

Mrs. Grant owned a small farm near St. Louis, and here he decided to try to make a living. He hewed logs and built a house, which he called "Hardscrabble."

A hard scrabble, indeed, did the army officer have in his efforts to make a farmer of himself.

In the spring he plowed the ground, and sowed and planted his grain; in the summer he mowed and threshed his wheat; and when winter came he gathered his corn, and cut wood to sell at four dollars a cord.

But in spite of his work he could not succeed, because he did not know how to manage. His horses and machinery cost so much, and the products of his farm brought so little, that, at the end of three years, he was two thousand dollars in debt.

The crops had to be sold, and the horses and implements put up at auction. The neighbors loitered about the place while the auctioneer called off the sales.

They found the stable well kept, and the horses in fine condition; Grant had learned how to do such work at West Point; but the thrifty farmers shook their heads when they saw that the plows were rusty and broken, and the grain bins were almost empty.

"Grant is a good fellow," they said; "but he was never cut out to be one of us!"

After everything was sold, Grant tried to get employment in St. Louis. He first went into the real estate business. He was so quiet and so shy that he could not make bargains. Then he tried to get an appointment as county engineer. He was too little known to the politicians, and so some one more favored than he received the office.

He worked in various ways to make a living for his family, but fortune seemed to frown upon him. When his father heard of his desperate straits he cast about to find how he might help him.

He wrote to a son who was in the leather business at Galena, Illinois, and told him of his brother's ill luck.

"Give Ulysses a chance, my boy," he said, "I may have spoiled him at West Point."

It was not long before Grant was clerking in the leather store at Galena. He was to receive only a few hundred dollars the first year. If he made a good salesman, his salary would then be increased. He went quietly about his tasks, and expected to be a leather merchant the rest of his life.

VII.—The War for the Union.

It was in the year 1860 that Grant went into the leather business. There was great excitement in Galena over the national conventions. Two citizens of Illinois, Stephen A. Douglas and Abraham Lincoln, were candidates for President of the United States.

One branch of the Democratic party nominated Douglas. The Democrats were then in power, with James Buchanan as President of the United States.

The Republican party nominated Lincoln. It was a new party, and had once been defeated.

If the Democratic party had been united Douglas would have felt sure of being elected. Lincoln was not sure about his own election; but he said that his party was in the right, and if it did not win this time it would the next. The chief question between the two parties was whether slavery should be allowed in the territories.

The United States owned several territories which had not yet been made into states. Douglas declared that the citizens of a territory had the right to say whether it should be a slave or a free state when it came into the Union.

Lincoln denied this. He said that the government of the United States had control of its territories before they became states. He quoted the Declaration of Independence—that all men are "endowed by their Creator with life, liberty, and the pursuit of happiness," and he said that Washington and Jefferson had intended that government land should be free soil.

Many of the people in the North agreed with Lincoln. "He is right," they said. "Look at Europe. Every respectable nation in Europe has set its slaves free. America boasts that she is the 'land of the free and the home of the brave,' and stamps *Liberty* on her coins, yet four million human beings are kept as slaves within her borders. We cannot prevent slavery in the old states, but let us forbid it in the new states."

In the end the Republicans elected Abraham Lincoln.

Before he was inaugurated, South Carolina seceded from the Union. Perhaps you will remember that, in 1832, South Carolina tried to secede from the Union and President Andrew Jackson prevented it by sending a warship to Charleston.

But James Buchanan was a very different kind of president. He allowed other states to join South Carolina. They established a government of their own which they called the Confederate States of America, with Jefferson Davis as president.

The members of Congress from the Confederate States; the secretaries in Buchanan's Cabinet; and many officers in the army and navy resigned their places and took oath to support the new government.

Most of the forts in the South, which belonged to the United States, were seized by the Confederates. The commander of Fort Sumter in Charleston Harbor was Robert Anderson. He was a brave soldier and had been wounded at Chapultepec while fighting by the side of Grant.

Major Anderson refused to surrender his fort. The whole world waited to see what Abraham

Lincoln would do when he became President. He was inaugurated on the 4th of March, 1861.

In his speech he said: " I shall take care that the laws of the Union be faithfully executed in all the states. In doing this there need be no bloodshed or violence, and there shall be none unless it be forced upon the national authority."

Very soon after this the Confederates again demanded the surrender of Fort Sumter. Major Anderson stoutly refused and kept the Stars and Stripes waving on the flagstaff. At last the Confederates fired on the fort.

When the people in the North heard that the flag of the Union had been dishonored, they forgot all about the slavery question and united to defend the honor of the United States government.

One young Democrat in Galena, who had voted against Lincoln for President, said : " I am not a Democrat now, nor a Republican, either; I am an American and will defend our flag!"

When President Lincoln called for 75,000 volunteers so many enrolled at Galena that a company was formed immediately.

Grant quit the leather store. He said: "The United States educated me for the army. What I am I owe to my country. I have served her through one war and, live or die, I will serve her through this."

He drilled the Galena company and helped them get their blue uniforms ready.

He was soon called to Springfield and made colonel of the 21st Illinois regiment of infantry. The men were disorderly. Their former colonel had been dismissed because he could not control them.

When Grant appeared before them on the drill-ground he was in citizen's dress. He looked shabby and seemed so modest that they began to jeer at him. "Speech! Speech!" they cried.

"Soldiers," said Grant, "go to your quarters." His tones were so commanding that they obeyed. It was not long before they said: "Grant knows what he is about. We can't scare him or deceive him."

The 21st regiment was ordered to Missouri to guard the railroads. Grant did not transport his troops on the cars. He knew they must become accustomed to long marches.

" My first marching should be in a friendly country," he said.

He drilled his men on the way to Missouri and taught them to obey every one of his commands.

At this very time the Confederates at Richmond, Virginia, were wondering who would be the officers in the armies of the North.

" There is one West Pointer," said General Beauregard, " whom I hope the Northern people will not find out; I mean 'Sam' Grant. I knew him well at West Point and in Mexico. I should fear him more than any other man they have. He is clear headed, quick, and daring."

VIII.—FORTS HENRY AND DONELSON.

It was not long until the Northern people *did* find out " Sam " Grant. After several skirmishes with the Confederates he was made brigadier-general with headquarters at Cairo, Illinois.

Missouri and Kentucky were still in the Union; but they were slave states.

" Missouri must be ours," said the Confederates;
" for the lead mines for our bullets are there, and
most of the slaveholders will help us."

They hurried guns and troops to Columbus, in
Kentucky, which stood on a high bluff overlooking
the Missouri shore.

" Kentucky must belong to us, too," they said.
" It must be our vanguard on the border of three
Union states."

They planted guns at Fort Henry on the Tennessee, and at Fort Donelson on the Cumberland,
and along the east bank of the Mississippi. Then
they stretched their armies from the great river to
the Atlantic ocean."

" The Yankees cannot invade the South by land
or water," said the men in gray.

" We must see about that," said General
Grant.

He laid plans with Commodore Foote who commanded the gunboats on the Ohio. Soon a fleet of
boats steamed up the Tennessee with transports.
Grant, with seventeen thousand men in blue, was
landed four miles below the fort.

And while the army marched by land, the gun-

boats proceeded up the river to the fort. Shot and
shell plowed through its earthworks and crippled
its mounted guns.

The Confederates saw that it was useless to try
to hold Fort Henry. They raised the white flag of
surrender. But the smoke was so dense it could
not be seen. The firing from the boats continued
and then two thousand Confederates fled in a panic
to Fort Donelson, twelve miles away.

In the meantime Grant was hurrying up with his
army as fast as he could. The ground was wet
from a heavy rain. His progress was so slow that
when he reached the fort, the Stars and Stripes
were waving on its flagstaff.

"Can you do as well as that at Donelson?" asked
General Grant of Commodore Foote.

"I shall do my best to help you take the fort,"
replied the brave seaman.

The Confederates were determined to hold Fort
Donelson. It guarded the Cumberland River,
which led up to Nashville, where their armies in
the West had headquarters. It was strongly in-
trenched on a bend of the river. Back of a line of
batteries at the water's edge were rifle pits; beyond

these were stretches of felled trees, and above all towered a broad bluff well guarded with cannon.

Grant marched toward the fort. The gunboats steamed down the Tennessee, then up the Ohio and then up the Cumberland. When Commodore Foote came near the fort he opened fire; but his shots were answered with shots from the batteries until nearly every gunboat was crippled.

The Union soldiers surrounded the fort, and for three days there was hard fighting. Then Grant secured a commanding position overlooking the fortifications. That night the Union army slept well. It was sure of victory on the next day.

But there was no sleeping in the great fort. Lights were moving all night long. Early next morning a negro came into the Union camp saying he had some news for " de gen'l."

" Dey's been a goin' all night! "

" What?" said Grant; "leaving the fort?"

" Yes, Massa, ef I's don't tell de truf I'll hang. Dey's been a goin' all night."

The old negro was right. Many Confederates had escaped under cover of the night.

General Buckner was in command of the fort.

He knew Grant well. He was the same Buckner that had been lost in a storm with him on Mount Popocatepetl, and he understood what kind of a person he had to oppose.

"It is useless to hold out against such a man as Grant," he said. "He will never retreat. I must surrender, but I'll get the best terms I can."

So he wrote a letter asking favorable terms. Grant promptly replied: "No terms, except unconditional and immediate surrender, can be accepted. I propose to move immediately upon your works."

General Buckner and fourteen thousand men laid down their arms as prisoners of war.

When the news of the fall of Donelson reached the North, people could hardly believe it.

" Who *is* this Grant? " they asked.

" I remember a little lieutenant who won laurels in the war with Mexico," said General Winfield Scott; "his name was U. S. Grant."

" The 'U. S.' stands for Unconditional Surrender!" said the delighted people.

Grant was soon afterwards made major general.

IX.—SHILOH, OR PITTSBURG LANDING.

After the surrender of forts Henry and Donelson the Confederates abandoned Columbus, Kentucky, and Nashville, Tennessee. They hurried to Corinth, a little town in northern Mississippi, where they collected large stores of food and ammunition. They planned to cross the Ohio and carry war into the North.

General Grant heard that a large army was collecting at Corinth.

" This army must not go North," he said to his generals.

He sent to Nashville for more troops and transported his army up the Tennessee to Pittsburg Landing, about twenty miles from Corinth. Here he went into camp while waiting for the Nashville troops. His lines stretched out several miles.

One night the Confederates marched from Corinth. General Albert Sidney Johnston was in command. He made a quick attack upon one wing of Grant's army at Shiloh Church, three miles from Pittsburg Landing.

It was just daylight. The cooks in the Union camp were stirring the camp fires for breakfast.

The arms were stacked and many soldiers were still asleep.

Shot and shell tore through the tents. Some were killed in their beds; some fled in a panic; but the most of the men seized their guns and made a bold stand.

Grant was several miles away when he heard the roar of the cannon. He took a boat for the front and was soon in the midst of the battle. The men fell, dead and wounded, around him; a ball struck the scabbard of his sword and broke it off; but he hurried from one company to another, urging them forward.

All day the battle raged. The Union army was driven slowly back to the landing. Despair was written on every face. Suddenly cheer on cheer arose. Buell's army from Nashville was seen on the opposite bank of the river.

Union gunboats hurled shells upon the pursuing enemy as evening came on; but the battle of Shiloh seemed won by the Confederates.

"What preparations have you made for surrender?" asked General Buell, as he sat with Grant in his tent.

"I have not given up hope of victory yet," replied Grant.

During most of the night he and his generals formed their lines for the morning.

Now the Confederates expected that the blue coats would be fleeing for safety down the river; but when the sun rose, there stood the Union army in battle array. The struggle began again. The Confederates were driven back until they had lost all they had won the day before. When night came on again, the Union troops threw themselves down on the ground to sleep. The Confederates returned to Corinth. In a few weeks they retreated from Corinth. Then Union troops and gunboats moved down the Mississippi River, defeated the Confederate ironclads and took possession of Memphis. The states north of the Ohio were safe.

Grant was given command of the Department of Tennessee and made his headquarters at Corinth.

X.—VICKSBURG.

All this time there had been fighting at the mouth of the Mississippi. Commodore Farragut ascended the river, bombarded the forts, and captured New Orleans.

Farragut then wished to join Grant up the river; but Port Hudson stood in the way.

Grant wished to join Farragut down the river; but Vicksburg stood in the way.

Between these two forts the Confederates had control of the country. They brought flour and cattle from Texas and Louisiana to feed their armies.

"No gunboats can pass Vicksburg without my consent," said General Pemberton whose army guarded the batteries along the waters edge.

"We'll see about that," said General Grant; "I think we shall now split the Confederacy in two, and the wedge that shall do it will be my army at Vicksburg."

He marched his troops from Corinth to Memphis, and, floating down the river, he landed a few miles above Vicksburg. Before him were high bluffs and a dense forest, bristling with guns. It was quite out of the question to reach the fort from the north.

"We must attack it from the south," said Grant.

" Impossible! " exclaimed his generals.

Vicksburg stood on a bend of the river and was guarded for eight miles with batteries. There seemed no way to carry provisions past the fort.

" We will coax the river to change its old bed," said Grant.

He set thousands of men to digging a broad canal across the neck of land opposite Vicksburg. They worked for several months.

But the summer sun melted the snows in the mountains. The Ohio, the Missouri, and the Arkansas rolled in floods into the Mississippi, and then the great river overflowed its banks and filled the canal. The troops were obliged to flee for their lives.

" Ha! ha! " cried men in the South. "Even the ' Father of Waters' is helping us."

"Shame! shame!" said men in the North. "Our armies are wasting time making ditches."

Some busy bodies went to Washington and said to President Lincoln: " Remove Grant from command and put a *real* general in his place."

But the President replied: "I rather like the man. I think I will try him a little longer."

Grant did not say a word when he heard about the complaints. He had his plans. He knew very well that if these plans failed he would be removed from command.

He called an old boatman to his tent. "Can I run my transports past the batteries on a very dark night?"

"It might be done, general; but it's a great risk you'd be taking."

"I'll take the risk," said Grant to himself.

He had a talk with Admiral Porter who commanded the gunboats, and then he crossed the Mississippi with his army. He marched down the west bank and halted south of Vicksburg.

The terrible fort now shut off supplies.

"Grant has put his army into a death trap!" cried his enemies in the North. Even President Lincoln thought perhaps he had made a mistake. But Grant's plans were not yet complete. He was waiting for Porter.

One very dark night three transports were made ready. They were fashioned wide and long to carry supplies. Their boilers were padded with cotton and wet hay that could not easily be pene-

trated by bullets; their engines were oiled that
every joint might work its best; and their fires
were screened that their light might be hid.

Then eight of Porter's gunboats sailed out, like
angry monsters, before Vicksburg. The transports
ran at full speed behind their shelter. The Confederate guards saw the gunboats. Bonfires were
built on the shore. It was as light as day on the
river. Shot and shell screamed through the air;
but on sped the provision boats, while Porter's
guns answered those on the shore.

One of the transports was burned; but the others
passed the batteries, followed closely by the gunboats. At daybreak the little fleet sailed up to
Grant's camp, on the west bank of the river; and
men and supplies were soon across the river.

Friendly negroes guided the army as it fought
its way toward Vicksburg. Pemberton, with his
troops, was soon shut up inside the city. A siege
was begun. Shot poured into Vicksburg until
the citizens had to dig caves and cellars for
shelter. Pemberton must have remembered the
cannonading in the belfry of the old church in
front of Mexico!

The weeks went by, and at last the Confederates were starving.

"We will escape by the river," said Pemberton.

Houses were torn down to build rafts; but the gunboats drove the rafts back.

"We will flee in the night by way of unfrequented roads," said Pemberton; but two hundred cannons were guarding those roads.

Grant's army lay coiled around the city like a huge serpent guarding its prey. And, at last, on the 4th of July, 1863, General Pemberton made an unconditional surrender.

When Admiral Porter saw the Union flag waving from the ramparts of the city, he hurried his gunboats beneath the friendly walls. And fleet and army celebrated Independence Day in Vicksburg.

"It's Grant again," said the people of the North, when they heard the good news. "It's Unconditional Surrender Grant!"

President Lincoln wrote: "My Dear General: I do not remember that you and I ever met personally. I write this now as a grateful acknowledgment for the almost inestimable service you have done the country."

Grant was given command of all the armies in the West.

XI.—CHATTANOOGA.

While Grant and other generals were fighting in the West, war had been raging in the East. Washington, the capital of the United States, and Richmond, the capital of the Confederate States, were both well guarded.

When Robert E. Lee became commander of the army at Richmond, he asked for more clothing and food for his soldiers.

"If General Lee wants supplies, let him find them in the North," said the Confederate commissary general.

Lee crossed the Potomac River and marched into Pennsylvania. He was met by General Meade at Gettysburg and driven back into Virginia, just one day before the surrender of Vicksburg.

"We must keep Lee in Virginia," said Grant when he heard of it.

He began to gather his forces together to march toward Virginia. On the line of march lay Chattanooga, where General Rosecrans, with a Union army, was shut up by the Confederates. There seemed no way for him to escape. On the north of the city was the Tennessee River, on the east, south, and west were high mountains, with cannons guarding all the passes.

"We must get the boys out of Chattanooga," said Grant. With Sherman, Sheridan, and other brave officers he led his armies to an assault.

They stormed up the mountain sides. Some of the fighting on Lookout Mountain was so high that the engagement is called the "battle above the clouds."

The Confederates were routed completely, and the starving army was fed. When the news of the victory at Chattanooga reached the North, there was the wildest excitement.

"Unconditional Surrender Grant has a better name now," cried the people. "It is Uniformly Successful Grant!"

Congress ordered a gold medal for the conqueror; and some congressmen said, "Washington fought for the independence of our states; Grant is fighting for their union. Washington was lieutenant-general of the army, let us revive the grade for Grant."

And so the hero was summoned North to receive his new title. Special trains carried him to Washington. At every station crowds gathered to see him. He bore his honors with modesty, and, when he reached the capital, went quietly to a hotel. Few persons knew that he was there.

While he sat unnoticed in the dining room a gentleman recognized him, and when it was whispered about who the stranger was, cheers resounded through the hall; he could hardly return to his room for the crowd.

Lincoln, when he handed him his commission as lieutenant-general, said: "As the country herein trusts you, so, under God, will it sustain you."

Grant felt very serious at that moment. It seemed that the success of the Union arms depended on his skill. And when some fashionable ladies of Washington wished to give a ball in his honor, he said: "Ladies, I wish to ask you, in all kindness, if this is a time for music and feasting among the officials of the army.

"Do dances soothe our sick and wounded?

Do they inspire our troops with courage in the field ?"

You may be sure that the ball was not given.

XII.—THE CLOSE OF THE WAR.

"We must work together," said Lieutenant-General Grant, "but we must keep the enemy divided."

He planned a campaign with General Sherman, and then hurried to the East to take command of the Army of the Potomac.

Sherman defeated the Confederates in the West, and then marched toward the sea. His army was in four columns covering a belt of country sixty miles wide. He destroyed bridges, railroads, and provisions, so that no aid could be sent to Lee at Richmond.

It was a terrible thing to do; but there seemed to be no other way of ending the war. When Sherman reached Savannah he went into winter quarters to wait until Grant might need him.

All this time Grant was fighting around Richmond. Some of the battles were in such a wilderness that the armies could not stand in line; but shot and shell shrieked through the gloomy shade. The loss of life was so frightful that many thought Grant should abandon the siege around Richmond.

But Grant said: "I propose to fight it out on this line if it takes all summer."

This was not because he was careless about the loss of so many brave soldiers. When news came that one gallant officer had fallen, he sat alone and sobbed. The whole army knew of his sorrow, and the band gathered at the door of his tent to play a funeral dirge.

The slaughter of battle was as dreadful to Grant as to any one else; yet he knew that the cruel war must be ended by desperate fighting.

At last his army surrounded Lee's army. On the 9th of April, 1865, Lee surrendered at Appomattox Court House, about seventy-five miles from Richmond.

The two generals met at a farm house to agree upon terms. Lee wore an elegant new uniform, with a sword at his side. Grant was in plain soldier's blouse, and without a sword. He did not

wish to make a display of authority before his
unhappy countrymen.

He gave generous terms of surrender. No men
were kept as prisoners, and all were allowed to
keep their horses.

"They will need them to work their little
farms," he said.

There was rejoicing in the North and in the
South that the conflict was over. But the joy was
turned to grief when President Lincoln was assas-
sinated. He had been Grant's best friend, and
it was with a sad heart that the victorious general
marched his army into Washington.

Vice-President Johnson had become President,
and before him the troops passed in review.
Then they went to their own states to return to
their shops and farms.

General Grant went to his home in Galena,
Illinois. The grateful people all over the country
raised large sums of money for him. The citizens
of Galena presented him an elegant house, and
those of Boston sent him a library of rare books.

Congress created for him the grade of General.
Even Washington did not receive such a high

military title as that. Then some began to say that
U. S. stood for " United States," and that it would
be a graceful act to make U. S. Grant President of
the United States.

XIII.—PRESIDENT OF THE UNITED STATES.

Andrew Johnson was a very unpopular President,
and when the time came for the national convention the Republicans nominated General Grant to
succeed him.

During the campaign which followed, he did not
go about making speeches.

" No terms except unconditional surrender."

" I shall fight it out on this line if it takes all
summer."

" The men will need their horses to work their
little farms."

" The people of the South are again our
countrymen."

" Let us have peace " —— These were some of
the speeches he had made during the four years'
war and the people remembered them.

They elected him President and he was inaugu-

rated March 4, 1869. His first term was so successful that he was elected for a second term.

When the year 1876 came, Congress decided to
celebrate the centennial of the Declaration of
Independence by giving a World's Fair.

You can guess why Philadelphia was chosen for
the Fair. All the foreign nations were invited.
Some said that the monarchs of Europe would not
take part in such a parade over the birthday of a
republic. But they did.

Even Queen Victoria sent laces and other
beautiful things to this Fair which celebrated the
day when our patriots refused to obey her tyranni-
cal grandfather.

The Centennial Exposition helped to unite the
people of the North and the South more than anything else had done since the war. Those from
South Carolina remembered how their forefathers
had sent rice to Boston when King George had
shut up her port. Those from Virginia recalled
how Patrick Henry had spoken in Philadelphia for
liberty and George Washington had fought for
liberty and Union.

The Fair lasted for six months; but, of course,

General Grant's Birthplace

Boyhood Home

Monument and Tomb.

House in 66th St.

the great day was the 4th of July. President
Grant was present then, and stood on a reviewing
stand while a grand procession passed. He
received the foreign guests with dignity, and won
the praise of all by his plain common sense.

The people were so proud of him that some
declared he must serve for a third term. But
Grant remembered the example of Washington
and Jefferson. He said : " I will not serve again.
There are many others as worthy as I."

Rutherford B. Hayes, of Ohio, was elected President and, after his inauguration, General Grant
returned to his home in Galena.

XIV.—THE TRAVELS OF ULYSSES.

It is said that after he had served his country all
he could, the Greek Ulysses wandered over the
known world; and that is just what his American
namesake did.

While Grant was President his only daughter,
Nellie, married an English gentleman. And now
that his public duties were over, he resolved to pay
her a visit. So he set sail from Philadelphia with
his wife and one son.

When Queen Victoria learned that Grant was coming to England she did not know just what to do. She asked her ministers: "Shall we receive him as a ruler or as a private citizen?"

Ex-presidents Martin Van Buren and Millard Fillmore had both traveled abroad as private citizens.

But just at this time Lord Beaconsfield was prime minister in England. He had once been a commoner yet he had more power at court than any nobleman in the realm. He said to the queen: "We will be doing honor to a wonderful general and pay a high tribute to a great nation if we receive ex-President Grant as a sovereign."

And so when Grant's steamer reached Liverpool, the flags of all nations were flung to the breeze in greeting. *Hail Columbia* and *The Star Spangled Banner* were played by the bands.

At Manchester, where the lack of cotton during the American war had stopped the humming of thousands of spindles, the name of Grant was well known.

When he made a speech to the delegates from the Labor Unions, he said: "In America we recognize that labor dishonors no man. No matter what a man's occupation is, he is eligible to fill any post in the gift of the people."

And who was better fitted than Grant, the tanner, to prove these words?

He was received in state at Windsor Castle by the queen, and the Prince of Wales did him honor.

Wherever Grant went he learned much about famous generals. In Sweden he saw the clothes of Gustavus Adolphus, stained with the blood of battle; in Germany he stood at the grave of Frederick the Great; in France he lingered over the tomb of Napoleon; in Spain he examined the armor of King Ferdinand; in Italy he admired the marble busts of the Cæsars; in Russia he held the sword of Peter the Great; in Egypt he climbed the pyramids of the Pharaohs. Wherever he went he heard of great generals and he knew that the world called him one of the greatest.

Yet when he entered Jerusalem and saw the tomb of Jesus of Nazareth, he said: " Here slept the real warrior! He conquered the world with his love." He stood a long time with bowed head at this tomb of the carpenter's son, whose mission was "peace on earth and good will to men!"

When Grant reached China, he thought that no one there would know anything about him. Yet at Shanghai he was received with fireworks. One of the banners in a procession said: "Washington, Lincoln, and Grant, three immortal Americans!"

The emperor of China was only eight years old and the prime minister, Li Hung Chang, received Grant at Canton. The two men became great friends. Grant urged the Chinese statesman to come to America to study modern methods of living.

At Nagasaki, in Japan, the Mikado shook his hand. Such an honor had never before been granted to a foreigner.

At last Grant set sail from Yokohama for home. When he reached San Francisco the harbor was crowded with steamers, yachts, and tugs. Thousands of his countrymen greeted him with cheers. Bands of music played national airs, and at night bonfires were built and sky-rockets lighted the sky.

Grant went back to Galena. After a time he moved to New York city; but wherever he lived he was loved and respected.

XV.—THE CLOSING YEARS.

General Grant lived in New York like any other private citizen. He invested his money in the banking business. He had wealth and friends and honor. It seemed that he would have nothing to do the rest of his life but enjoy himself.

But the year that he was sixty-two years old misfortune came. The manager of his bank proved dishonest. Grant found himself deprived of his fortune. He fell ill. Throat trouble developed. When he was able to be about again some publishers asked him to write for a magazine.

He said he was not sure that he could write anything worth reading, but he would try. He wrote about the battle of Shiloh.

Everybody wanted to read what the hero of Shiloh had written. The publishers were delighted. They asked him to write more; and he wrote about the siege of Vicksburg.

Meanwhile his throat was growing worse. One morning the doctors looked very grave. They told him he could live only a few months.

Grant had never surrendered in any battle; yet he knew that Death conquers all. He wanted

very much to live long enough to pay his debts
and make his family comfortable.

And so he began to write what he called his
Memoirs. Most of the book was to be about the
civil war. His throat pained him ; he grew thin
and pale ; but he worked away at his task. He
became so weak that he was removed to Mount
McGregor, near Saratoga.

News came to him that many thousand people
had subscribed for his book. This pleased him
very much. At last, the *Memoirs* was finished.
He laid down his pen and, a few days later, on the
23d of July, 1885, he died.

His body was carried to the city hall in New
York, where it lay in state. Thousands passed to
view the remains.

Almost all who passed had lost a relative or a
friend in the war, and they felt that General Grant
had gone to meet his comrades on the great
recruiting ground on high.

He was borne to a temporary vault on the
banks of the Hudson.

Among the pall-bearers were General Buckner,
whom he had conquered at Fort Donelson,

and General Joseph E. Johnston, once the commander of Confederate armies.

These heroes from the South walked side by side with other heroes from the North.

A temple of pure white marble was erected in Riverside Park for his last resting place. Among those who contributed funds to build it was Li Hung Chang in far-away China.

In 1897, when the Chinese prime minister came to New York, he was borne to the tomb in his sedan chair. He stood long in silence at the sarcophagus which enclosed the remains of his friend.

And every day in winter, when the snow lies cold around the marble tomb, and in summer, when the banks of the Hudson gird it with green, people enter within the noble monument and stand in silence before the remains of Ulysses S. Grant, the protector of our American Union ; and with solemn thoughts they read the inscription, Grant's own words, carved in the white stone above the doorway :—

"LET US HAVE PEACE."

www.ingramcontent.com/pod-product-compliance
Lightning Source LLC
Chambersburg PA
CBHW031428020726
47499CB00005B/1647